To Herbert.
For developing a son into a success through your positive influence.

"I can get a good look at a T-bone by sticking my head up a bull's ass, but I'd rather take a butcher's word for it." ~ Tommy Boy

What People Are Saying About Next in Line Please

"Jim Serger tells a wonderful story of fear, risk, hard work, failure and success. It's a story to which anyone who has ever chased a dream can relate. Mr. Serger not only tells a good story, he makes you pause and think. Who gave you the courage to chase your dream? Who ingrained in you the work ethic to make that dream a reality? Is there a parent, teacher or past employer you want to thank for believing in you? Maybe most importantly, who are you positively influencing to chase their dream? For those who have taken the leap to follow their dream, this book is a great way to remember how you became who you are, and motivate you to help others achieve their own success story."

Joe Santorelli --co-owner Arthur's restaurants; Hyde Park and Anderson.

"Jim Serger teaches sound principles of success discovered through the experience called life. A worthwhile read!"

John G. Miller, author of QBQ!, Outstanding!, and Parenting the QBQ Way

"Next In Line Please"

What a Butcher Can teach us about positive influence.

Jim Serger

"NEXT IN LINE PLEASE"

WHAT A BUTCHER CAN teach us
ABOUT POSITIVE INFLUENCE.

Jim Serger

Red Bike
PUBLISHING

Next in Line Please - What a Butcher Can Teach Us About Positive Influence

Published by: Red Bike Publishing
Copyright © 2016 by Jim Serger

Published in the United States of America
www.redbikepublishing.com

Red Bike Publishing also publishes books in electronic format. Some publications appearing in print may not be available in electronic book format.

Library of Congress Control Number: 2015960949
ISBN: 978-1-936800-15-5

CONTENTS

FORWARD

SUMMIT MEATS

A funny thing happen to me when I got to the airport. A few days earlier a high school friend, Jim Serger, had called and told me he was writing a book about my dad and he wanted me to write the forward. Jim said he would need to the forward in about two weeks' time but my problem was that I was traveling non-stop for the next two week. My only chance to read Jim's book was on my flight to Minneapolis. However my flight was taking place on 9/11/15 so Jim's book was not on my mind when I got to the airport. My other distraction was that I knew I would be flying over thunderstorms to get to Minneapolis and having already been on 2 flights struck by lightning, well I was a little nervous about my day's travel.

So I parked my car in the long term parking lot at the airport and hopped on the shuttle which was surprisingly full. As we were about to depart to the terminal a husband and wife jumped on the bus at the last minute. There was barely enough room for one of them to sit and the husband showed no inclination to find a seat. As soon as I realized there really wasn't enough room for the wife to sit I stood up and offered her my seat. As the son of Bob Cappel I was raised to give up my seat to any women in need of one. I can think of countless times at family gatherings where my dad would tell me to get up from my seat so one of my aunts could sit down. After a while you stop needing to be told and just do it.

So with all of my concerns about my day's travel and knowing I had to read Jim's book, here I am doing what my dad had taught. Only this time I would remember why it was that I got up to offer my seat. How many times do we do the right thing but not think about why we are doing them or how we learned how to do them? Jim does an excellent job in this book showing how my dad always put his customer first. What I can tell you is that it was not just the customers he put first. I can honestly say my dad is the most selfless person I have ever met. He always thinks about the other person and what he can do to help them. When he asks someone how they are doing, he honestly wants to know and isn't just making small talk.

As for the author, I have known him on and off most of my life. The thing that I will always remember about Jim is his loyalty as a friend. I graduated from a very small grade school and knew few people at my new high school, Archbishop McNicholas. And while I did not know Jim personally at the start of my Freshman year, Jim knew my dad. Jim was a multiple sport athlete and already knew most of the kids in the school. I was a 5'4", 118 pound moving target for upperclassman. With that being said, if Jim ever saw anyone pick on his friends, he would step in immediately. I always knew Jim had my back, even though we didn't know each other that well yet. That would all change in Father Ed's religion class when Jim and I sat next to each other. I know that I had more conversations with Jim that year than I did lessons learned in class. Sorry Father Ed, but I think you would agree everything worked out for the best.

I really enjoyed reading Jim's book. There are many themes within that I agree with including the value of working at a young age. If Jim's book did anything for me it is to remind me what I already knew. I am proud to be a friend of Jim Serger and even more proud to be the son of Bob Cappel.

Kevin Cappel

PREFACE

We all gaze back keenly on our upbringing from time to time. It seems like today at forty-four I do quite a bit. I will be conducting a meeting and a fond memory stored way back there in my mind will just burst right to the front and without hesitation, I will tell a tale about people, coaches, teachers and businesses owners who have shaped my existence into what it is today.

Why is it that I adore speaking with people? Why is it that I get to work a half hour to an hour before I am scheduled? Why is it that I have only called in under the weather one time in the past thirty years? Why is it that I will labor on weekends, I will work Christmas, I will hustle on Super Bowl Sunday without complaining? Okay, I will gripe internally, but not to others. Why is it that I will still go to work knowing that I am sick? (I won't tell anyone). Why is it that I can work sixty days consecutively and not protest? What motivates me to get up at 2 am, read a book and leave for work at 4:00 am, get to work at 4:30, chat with the team, check my email and then initiate the day at 5am like I am supposed to? Why is it I know all the names of the people on my squad; if they are married or not, how many kids they have, where they went to school, where they were born, what vehicle they drive, their preferred football team, desired food?

Why is Jim Serger willing to stand up and offer his seat to a woman, when clearly there are no seats left while riding the shuttle bus from the employee parking lot to the airport terminal? Why do people approach me and ask for advice that has nothing to do with their occupation? Why do I hold the door open for a lady and for a guy? The guys give me a weird look, but that is okay. I just say my grandma would be proud of me. Why is it that I give a firm hand shake, look people in the eye? Why is it that I love to vacuum at work, when clearly I am in a suit and tie. Why is it, when I initiate a meeting I ask trivia questions; to conclude the meetings I ask trivia questions and if you get it right, you get to depart first? What are the grounds for me cooking breakfast for the workforce and preparing walking-taco day for the staff? Why is it that before I did a charter for the Golden State Warriors basketball team, I shoveled the snow in front of the building? Clearly that was not my post. My employees even interacted and said "Jim, that is not your job." My reaction was you are accurate, it's not mine. I completed it anyway.

Now, to respond to all of those questions, you have to go way back and I mean way back to when I was a youngster. My parents groomed me to be respectful of others. To shake hands. To converse with others. To hold the doors for others. To clean up after myself. To say hi to strangers. Yes, strangers in passing. To give a smile. To say good morning, good afternoon and good evening. My parents are so influential to me. Today at forty-four and being a operations manager at the Indianapolis Airport all of the interactions with people have built me up to where I am currently. I give credit to my parents who I adore and respect. Because of them   I am not intimidated at all to introduce myself to anybody. That confidence has been with me through playing sports all throughout high school and umpiring baseball games as a teenager. My dad encouraging me to go shovel snow for the neighbors at eleven. My mom asked me to lend a hand for grandma and grandpa. Christmas lights and cleaning up their yard. My parents would applaud me for all of my early endeavors.

Positive influence has shaped my life; from the University of Cincinnati to Delta Tau Delta fraternity house and, of course, my four year stint in the Navy. The interaction with others has molded me into who I am. That stems from people I intermingled with, who also had the "positive influence spell" placed on them. It is a forever ripple effect. The ripples keep going and going on for infinity, as long as we can comprehend. We all have influence over others. Good and bad; but it's up to us to align ourselves to the force, instead of over to the dark side. Positive role models produce positive influence. We all are role models. We just need to realize all are watching our every move. As a young teenager, managers shape us, teachers and coaches cast us, friends style us and, of course, our parents most of all form us. What about those who we meet for the first time. The ones who take us under their wing and direct us through their fellowship and through their leadership skills. The ones who have a large impact, but in a small way.

At sixteen years old, I obtained my first beloved job with a convenience store in Cincinnati, Ohio. The minute I became employed, it just seemed to click. I respected it and I continued to work there for 6 years, through high school and college. It was in an unbelievable spot, located in a tiny strip mall. Convenient Food Mart was the anchor store, right in the middle. To the left was a butcher shop, Summit Meats. To the right, was Domino's Pizza and down at the other end was Cincinnati Federal Savings and Loan. Each business served a purpose in my life as a teenager. Yes, I worked at Convenient Food Mart, but I interacted with the other three daily, weekly, and sometimes hourly.

As an adolescent we really don't comprehend the present. We are always wanting to be grown-up, be in college, have a superior car. We don't realize what is transpiring around us; school, football, dances, work, parties. All seem to be at the center of our existence. As we get older (in my case forty-four) we tend to glance back and see really why we are who we are. The community who we thought was tough on us was really cheering us on. The ones holding us accountable were the ones who knew our potential. The ones who explained work ethic, saw us as a future leader.

At the top of this introduction I went through a series of questions that I ask myself all the time. Believe me, there is a whole encyclopedia of other questions I ask myself. Those are just a few examples of how I carry myself today and I do my best to teach my daughter the same concepts; she volunteers at ten, she shovels snow at ten, she reads, she enjoys meeting new people, she loves attempting new challenges and loves trivia and knowledge of new information.

But the question is, why is Jim Serger outgoing? Why is Jim Serger's work ethic so strong? Why doesn't Jim call in sick, why does he show up early? The answer is this; Jim was taught at a young age to work hard, show up on time and be accountable.

This book is about what I learned from a butcher, not the convenient store I worked for, but the butcher shop next door. I am in customer service and I have been all my life. I have an enthusiastic understanding of what it takes to thrive in the business of putting others first. I was molded and shaped to put others first. My parents, business owners schooled me, shared with me and pushed me to improve each day.

At first, this manuscript was going to be a customer service paperback, the art and craft of putting others first. I had just released my book 2000 Miles on Wisdom, and wanted to dig deeper into my roots on why I grasp the notion of customer service. So I reached out to the butcher (who this book is about) and spoke with him about the notion of writing a book on customer service. However, the book quickly took a different route after interviewing him and swapping stories numerous times. The notion of opening a business, being in business and the impact of owning a store took center stage over a customer service book. This butcher had educated me so much about customer service that I wanted to manufacture a case of why he was in business in the first place.

So this book is not just about customer service, it's about being prepared for life. It's about being cheered on as a young man or women by our elders. It's about creating a path that will layout our journey and the trek we will take to create who we are. This book is a reflection of a man who went from zero understanding to owning a business. It's about his final destination, his career path and what made him a success. I am strong because of this man, I am grateful for this man and I appreciate this gentleman the older I get.

This volume is intended to allow ourselves to observe through the eyes of another business owner, the steps he took to attain brilliance. It didn't ensue overnight, so if you want to read what it takes to have an impact on a community, have an impact on your staff, have an impact on others through a business, then let's carry on.

I have heard over the years about students walking to school; the 1920's, 1930's, 1940's, 50's and 60's. My grandma told me numerous stories. What was so grasping about the story was that she had to stroll through the snow and through the extreme heat. It always sounded as if it was complete torture. I never walked to school, but I did walk home from school; detention. Yes, detention.

Now imagine this, a young boy, growing up in Cincinnati. A young son, who now is considered a baby boomer. A young ten year old, with a good solid Catholic upbringing. Good morals, excellent values, with a strong and ethical family living in a close-knit community. The communities we see now housed by young college grads and second generation occupants. The communities with the space between the homes so minute, a Smart Car would not fit through it. The communities where the homes were built on top of one another. Yet, these communities are making a comeback here in 2015. Why is that? Easy to respond. One, land is expensive so builders are cramming homes in any space available. Second is the notion of a community that we want to comprise. The communities where folks knew their neighbors, where a salt run was not to the store, but over to the neighbor's house for a pinch. In these dwellings were a tight set of values. Families knew families. People knew neighbors' names, knew their occupations, knew their work schedules. They understood fathers served in the war, understood the meaning behind "yes, sir." They understood the meaning of watching your back and keeping the family sacred. Helping thy neighbor.

It was a time of post war, a time of when having any occupation was seen as a fine job. Seen as a way of supplying income to a family. Whether they liked or not, dads tolerated their job. 9-5. Saturday and Sunday off. Church on Sunday, and a family get together on Sunday afternoons. The get-togethers where everything was prepared from scratch, where effort meant something, and where it seemed the days would by no means end. Lawn jarts were still acceptable to play, badminton was seen as cool, croquet was seen as a fun family game and where having two cars was seen as living the life of luxury.

It was the last 40's and the war had ended. Having a job, raising kids, having a roof over your head was seen as the norm. No extras! On a bread run, all change was given back to the parents. A coke was seen as a want and not a need, as it is today. Just plain old coffee was a thrill, instead of Starbucks. Baseball cards with the gum was still seen as safe. Jumping through the sprinkler was considered a water sport.

Principles were a norm. I work at an airport and today it looks as if passengers just awoke and began to scurry for the gates. There is no esteem for themselves or for others; hair in disarray, sweatpants on, flip flops, no compassion, no hellos, no thank you, no ethics or admiration for their fellow man. They throw a fit when their plane is delayed by 5 minutes, they throw a tantrum when the Starbucks line is too lengthy. They don't tip the skycaps, they don't tip the wheelchair pushers, they are so focused on their own needs, never considering others. They park their car in front of the airport unattended and when the police tow their car, they cuss up and down the curb. As if a five year old lost a lollipop. Yet, if there was a terrorist attack with a car unattended, they would be the first ones to raise a fit, question the protocol and say why did that happen? Yet, for them it seems okay.

The baby boomer generation is going to retire here soon. Well, let me rephrase that. They should retire soon. It seems as if though they may not. Their work ethic is off the charts. They understand tough times, sacrifice, saving money, what it means to be in a pinch and they understand not to spend when rewarded a good cash sum. They store it in a mattress for rainy days. The boomers will retire, but they will be in the game of labor. Volunteering, meals on wheels, tutor, coaches or whatever their passion is. The boomers love work. They understand the value of working and understand that work is a way of life; a necessity to living a active life. It's not that they have to work, it's because they want to work, because of positive influence over them at young age.

The gentleman I am going to talk about in this novel is man with sincerity. A man on a mission and a man who understands the significance of hard work. Not simply as it applies to his industry, but how he exemplifies good character, community interaction, connecting(now networking) with the local neighborhood, local grade schools, and local high schools. The thought of owning a business is scary. The dream of owning a business is the American way. But a dream is just that, a dream. Opening the doors is a whole new ball game, it's seen for only a select few. Well I am here to inform you that is a bunch of hogwash. We all can possess a business, but to own a successful business is a entire different category.

So as we progress into this script, envision yourself owning a corporation. Owning a LLC, or if you are a proprietor, what can you learn from a butcher. Yes, a butcher. Being an owner is more than making money; it's passion, it's leadership, it's commitment and it's being an expert. The chief payoff is creating positive influence over others, thus creating additional leaders. Store or no store, we all can have a influence over others.

"Opportunity is missed by most people because it is dressed in overalls and looks like work."

Thomas A. Edison

CHAPTER 1 10,000 HOURS

EXPERT

What is 10,000 hours? That is exactly the amount of time it seems to be considered an expert in your field or endeavor. Why 10,000 hours? The answer is this, you have a MD and you are cleared to perform surgery. Yet, as a surgeon each case is different; gunshot, head trauma, severed limb and each shift requires understanding of what is going to happen. Late at night alcohol accidents go up, early in the morning commuter accidents go up. Fourth of July, firework accidents go up. Snowing out, heart attacks go up. Sunny out, heat exhausted goes up. Each day brings on new cases that the surgeon had never seen or dealt with. Yet he/she understands the severity of the case, yet different cases come and go. We learn from each case, we learn from each interaction. Some for the good and some from the not so good. Doctors are under extreme pressure and an extremely tight time line. So as a physician, they develop to handle each case and each scenario.

So as the 10,000 hours progress, so does the expertise of being a doctor, thus turning them into superior surgeons. They have been educated on how to handle patients more meticulously and understand the flow of the ER and the hospital. Receiving a doctorate diploma is grand. Placing it over their mantle and gazing at it, so what. Effort comes after earning a degree. What you choose to do with it creates the expert. We prepare ourselves for the future. Dr. S earned his pre-med, med school and residency. Now off to get started understanding the material firsthand outside of the classroom. It's for real. No practice. Dr. S is a doctor, but, he must get in his 10,000 hours in one field to be an expert in that spectrum.

With a title comes responsibility. It comes with doing our finest and giving 100% each day. Not 50, 40, 60, 30%. But 100% into our occupation. I first heard of the 10,000 hour concept in the book, The 1% Solution by Tom Connellan. In the book, published in 2011, he states that in order to be the greatest you must have 10,000 hours of deliberate practice. He goes on to allocate; "Too many people who have been around for 30 years don't have 30 years experience. They have one year's experience 30 times."

In the book he places 5 keys as to being the best.
- To become the best of the best takes 10,000 hours of deliberate practice.
- Everyone who spends time in a deliberate practice improves their performance.
- Turn daily tasks into deliberate practice.
- Compare yourself to you, rather than to others.
- Plan ahead and set goals, but do your best in the present.[1]

The next book I read, also released in 2011, was Outliers, by Malcolm Gladwell. He spoke on a group who my parents grew up with, The Beatles. He stated that back in 1960 The Beatles went to Hamburg, Germany. They were still a very juvenile band and very much so undercompensated. Yet they went there to perform in the local clubs. Now to make matters poorer, the acoustics were dreadful and the audience could care less about them, yet they got hours of playing time. Hours of on stage performance and hours and hours of practice. They were yet to be heard of when arriving on the scene in Germany, yet they kept at it. By 1962, they were in demand, they were being spoke of and talked about. The Beatles were playing eight hours per night, seven days a week and by the time 1964 rolled around, The Beatles had over 1,200 concerts performed as we know The Beatles to be. The author goes on to state that by today's standards, most bands haven't even played 1,200 concerts in a life time.[2]

HUSTLE

I am going to share a stat with you on why the best of the best, is still not the greatest. My hero as a young child was Pete Rose. Charlie Hustle or as he puts it, "The Hit King."

Pete Rose played 24 years in the majors and collected 4,256 career hits. That is gigantic, considering he made 15,890 career plate appearances. So he complied a hit based on every 3.3 plate appearances, which is awesome to say the least. That is why he is the greatest. He collected a ton more plate appearances comparing him to another ball player with roughly the same amount of years in the big leagues.

Rick Dempsey, who played for 24 years, was a superb ball player. But, this is where we separate the good from the great. Rick only collected 5,407 plate appearances, which then produced only 1093 hits. This relates to getting a hit every 4.9 at bats.

So if we are using the 10,000 rule correctly; Pete Rose reached 10,000 plate appearances, plus achieved 4,053 more plate appearances than what is considered great. Rick was good, but he never reached the 10,000 mark. Does that make him still good? Absolutely, but we are not comparing success vs. average. We are comparing, why are the greatest the greatest, and why are the good just good. To be a ball player you must be great, but when comparing peers against peers, Pete Rose stood out that much more.

Why is it that Pete Rose achieved more? Is it because he was groomed to hustle it out from a early age by his dad? Was he told to hustle, to crave it more, to give it his all. To place it all on the field every single day, day in and day out. Pete knew he was good. To detach himself from the rest, he ran full sprint to first base, thus, beating out throws that were routine outs for other players. Pete created his own luck.

If Pete beat out every routine grounder once every eleven at bats, he would generate 1,441 hits just by beating out the throw. He forced others to hustle when he was playing. He forced his peers to give 100% because he was giving 100%.....The Reds won back to back World Series. He was a 17 time All-Star, NL MVP, NL Rookie of the Year. The hits just kept coming. Pete was prepared and he never settled for second best. That is why he is a part of the Major League All-Century Team.

Being the best is considered very flattering, but you must be humble about it. Being prepared for life sets one up to succeed. We all make choices. We all are guided down a path to a fork in the road we must choose. Without guidance, kinship, friends, and love, dreams and visions are just images. Seeing ones future and laying down tracks to get there is how I see the 10,000 hour principle. We just don't purchase a corporation and hope it works out. I can share with you numerous companies that have failed because of that philosophy. The 10,000 hour rule is simple. You are an expert in your "field" of business. You have seen it all, been through it all. You do not fake it until you make it. You make it because you did not fake it. A man reaps what he sows. Your roots have taken hold and your vision has grown year after year. You have fully matured and others seek your wisdom and guidance. You are the go to person. You are sought after for advice. Your answers are solid. People bet on you and your recommendations are never questioned. Staff glance at you with wide eyes. Customers rave about you. Peers thank you and young starlings follow you. You are considered deluxe in your occupation. So how did you achieve that?

There is a great book called QBQ, by John Miller. QBQ means; question behind the question. In this question of, how did you get to be so good? It should read, what seeds did you plant at a young age to acquire the skills you have today? When looking into the past of an astute business man, one must dig deep. Look way beyond what is on the surface. Look below the water line of an iceberg. We only see the tip. Below is the real answer.

As we turn the page and relinquish the butcher's name, the butcher's work ethic and the butcher's background, I want you as the reader to remember that this book was written because he had a impact on my life. He taught me ethics I use today, terminology I speak of today, and because of him, a small percentage of my accomplishments are due to his influence on me as a teenager.

According to Parents.com, there are five **values** parents must teach their kids by the age of five:

- Honesty
- Justice
- Determination
- Consideration
- Core[3]

COMMITMENT

It's very interesting that at age five we already know values that set us up for life. This book is about standards, beliefs and business astuteness a butcher shared with me and the thousands of local community folks he encountered in his life time. What is the difference between ham and eggs? The chicken is involved, but the pig is committed. He is a success because he was taught at a young age the value of commitment to work. The 10,000 hour principle had him prepared and ready to flourish. Because he was the pig, he was committed to achieving success.

10,000 hours to master your craft.

That's:

**8 hours a day
5 days a week
44 weeks a year
for 5 and half years.
Better get started**

Jacky Sherman.

CHAPTER 2 WALKING TO WORK

As I alluded to earlier, I spoke on the tight-knit communities that were running all over the United States. A time where a young boy could walk to school and still feel safe. I am sure there were a few local bullies as there are today; in the 60's you just didn't put up with them. You stood your ground, protected girls and walked tall. A few fist fights were seen as a good thing. They built character and strength.

Parents

The post WWII period never really left. Children were still were being told by their parents if you want something, you have to go get it. This time period, the 60's, is where kids could get a job, be creative and actually work. Moreover, it was a time where parents encouraged their kids to work, to be involved, to have a impact on their community and they started them off at an early age.

Bob Cappel is his name and yes, he walked to work, he rode his bicycle to work and I am sure he did it in the rain, snow, sleet and hail.

Bob Cappel was a normal everyday boy, growing up on the east side of Cincinnati in the community of Mt. Washington on Brachman Street. Bob had a durable, working father in the insurance field and a stay at home mother, plus he had 5 sisters. Bob enjoyed baseball and enjoyed running around the community with his friends. But what Bob did then is different than what young kids do today. Bob was interested in learning, growing and setting up his life for years of success. The only catch was Bob did not know it. Bob was a go getter in the scheme of work, but Bob did not see work as work. Bob saw employment as a way to get ahead, as a way to craft a buck and save. A way to have a bank account with money in it. He saw it as a means of planning for his opportunity, but he also saw labor as enjoyment, challenging and, yes, lucrative.

The reason Bob had this yearning to thrive at an early age was because his parents encouraged him to do more to balance his life. Focus on school, work a few days, play hard and have friends. Board games were the in piece; Monopoly, War, and card games were huge. Kids learned math soundly because of playing cards. Today, kids have no clue how to play cards, it's seen as a negative thing to notify people your son or daughter knows poker, yet back then, math scores were way up compared to today's scores. Bring back the card tables and set aside the Wii console. Bob was a typical youngster, growing up in a strong Catholic family, growing up surrounded by aunts and uncles, surrounded by family and friends. Bob was creative, but had the early stages of an entrepreneur because of watching his dad put forth a ton of sweat seven days a week, answering calls on weekends and late at night. Bob was born in 1949, and as a young boy, he was soaking up what effort meant through his dad, Herbert. His parents remembered the depression era and Cincinnati was no different than New York. Jobs were scarce. Soup lines and multiple families living under one roof. Herbert knew how crucial a job was and protected it with everything he had. He took ownership of his job and having to provide for his family was going to take extreme focus. Effort was habitual. Effort was every day. Effort was constant.

Lead

As a little boy, Bob watched his father. His eyes watching and learning from what he thought was an authority, his dad. He listened to his dad chat with customers on the telephone. Watched his dad fill out insurance forms. Watched his dad shake hands, watched his dad put in extensive hours. Yet, still watched his dad take time for his family. Herbert understood sacrifice. His family was sacred, but some nights he was unable to make the ball game or the dance recital. Herbert understood the insurance practice. Timing is everything. People had to work. House visits and business appointments were spread throughout different times of the day to accommodate the consumers needs. Bob was grasping the impression of organization, from his first real leader; his father.

Bob and his five sisters were raised in an era where the mom stayed home, and as it is today, it's a full-time post. Marie was her name, she never had an outside trade, but being a mom is a job. Yes, she dabbled in girl scouts, setting up dances at the school, conducting church events and the motherly tasks, but her job was being at home. Taking care of the six children so Herbert could conduct his job wisely and as efficiently as possible. We are influenced outside of our parents and Bob was no different. Bob's first encounter outside of parents and school was a childhood friend's dad, the one who would mold Bob.

MANAGER

Bernie Hornschemeier was his name. Bernie was the title-holder of his own company, a grocery store, Hornschemeier Grocery. A New York style store where you could get everything you needed within reason in a one stop shop. Bob would hop on his bike and ride up there and work alongside his friend, Dan, who was the son of Bernie. Dan and Bob would go to grade school together at Guardian Angels and would continue high school together at McNicholas. Both are excellent Catholic institutes. Bob and Dan were running mates; they labored alongside each other, went on double dates with each other, played baseball on the same teams, went to Coney Island, went to Reds games at old Crosley Field. But what made their affiliation extraordinary was that they both worked healthy together at a young age. They both were on the farm team, way down at the bottom of the independent leagues of business.

In 1965, while still in high school Bob and Dan would continue to work as a team and Bernie was right there encouraging them both to learn the ropes of the store. So as a young man, Bob began to understand the theory of owning a store, operating the cash register, learning to stock shelves, learning to order materials, and the magical part was, learning and functioning in the meat department. Yes, selling toilet paper was too simple. It was not very challenging to comprehend. When the paper was out, you just re-supply. The meat department, now that was taxing.

PSYCHOLOGY

There are common fears to we humans, we mortals. Speaking and death are right there at the top. Those standout, but then there are business oriented fears. Fears to overcome. Ones that set the stage for a successful career in entrepreneurship. But what I found were a few that just blew me away. Ergophobia, the morbid fear of returning to work. Ego-death, the fear of humiliation. Xenophobia, the fear of strangers. Acrophobia, the fear of stressful situations. Sociophobia, the fear of socializing. Bibliophobia, the fear of books and the last is Kleptophobia, the fear of stealing.

BELIEF

When we are young and encouraged to do well, the potential is infinite. We have instructors and coaches, other parents and, of course, our first manager. In Bob's case, it just so happened to be his best friend's dad. Talk about a door open concept. It fell right into Bob's lap. Yet, at a young age and in the 60's, Bob would follow Bernie's lead through the store. Bernie was guiding him and giving him massive responsibility as a teenager, which gave Bob the courage to do well.

We all have a choice to listen to our elders or rebel. Bob chose to take note. Bob chose to take the reign and go down a path that would lead him to greener pastures. The part so common to young adults is they don't spot their own potential. The elders do.

We all have been to a convenience store. We all have been to a grocery store and we all have been to the meat department. When was the last time you witnessed a teenager working in the meat department? When was the last time you saw someone under the age of 20 in the meat department? When was the last time you saw anyone under the age of 20 multitasking in a store? If you have, then you are in the minority, and if you were lucky enough to have been that person yourself, ask yourself how many years ago was that? What I mean by this, is the proposal of ownership for getting a profession, for having a job is remarkable. To love your job is even healthier, and as I will lay down the course in this book, that Bob loved his job because once again a gentleman set him up to look forward to coming to work. Bernie believed in Bob. He encouraged Bob and Bob felt that empathy.

Challenge

The porterhouse and sirloin steak, corned beef, pot roast, chicken breast, meatloaf, beerwurst, baked ham, pastrami, roast beef, pork roll, pepperoni, liverwurst, krakowska, salceson, smoked meat, American cheese and the list goes on and on. As a young lad, Bob was right there at the age of 18 in the meat department of Hornschemeier Grocery. The key word is "young". Bob was being molded for future endeavors, yet it still was Bob's choice to work there. No one was making him do it. Bob pursued it. But why? It was a time when having a job at a young age was seen as benefitting society. Parents at the time still remembered the great depression, still remembered the stock market crash, still remembered watered down milk, still remembered pinching pennies and those stories resonated with young adults. Work hard, provide for yourself, take care of yourself, do it yourself. If you want a car, you buy it. If you want new shoes, you buy it. Bob was right there. In the year 1965.

Walking to work. Yes, I know we have heard how back in the day people walked. Well, there was no obesity, so maybe that message needs to be screamed from the roof tops. But in Bob's case walking to work was only a few blocks as was walking to school. If you have ever been to Manhattan, the same structure takes place. Everything is within walking distance. No need for a license or a vehicle. A bicycle for sure, but no car insurance or gas. Seems as if they were saving and not even realizing it. Today we want that feeling, but we thought bigger was better. Now we want to turn the clock back and build what we once had, small tight communities with one stop shopping, in and out.

Explaining

Have you ever faced a store? Well have you? What is facing a store?

No it's not standing in the front and looking at the building. It's moving all the items on the shelves forward by date so the older ones sell first before the new shipment arrives. As a grocery store owner, that is the #1 concept of watching your P&L statements. Out of date food; canned food, milk, meat and produce will destroy a business. That rotation falls on everyone at the store; from the cashier, to the clerk, to the stock boy, to the meat department and to the dairy cases as well as frozen food cases. As a store proprietor, P&L is without hesitation the make or break concept. You, as the owner, have got to repeat the severity of watching your product. Bernie, by all means, explained the magnitude of this to Dan and Bob. Both young stock boys, young clerks in their white aprons; yet receiving the information and following Bernie's guide, turned Bob into a businessman. Understanding the tiny details that make a grocery store thrive and make customers want to come back. Giving a reason for the consumer to give repeat business.

Bob, would walk home from work feeling satisfied with his day's work, leaving work as if he was in charge, feeling the warm glow of his face as he ventured down the street, feeling a sense of accomplishment on the job. Knowing that tomorrow he will walk down again and learn more, gain more perspective on how to cut a steak, crank out some more sausages and sharpen the knives.

CHAPTER 3 OWNERSHIP OF THE JOB

DEVELOPMENT

What is ownership? That one word elevates a person from the rest of the pack. It separates the good from the great. But what is great? Great to me means that you and you only are willing to step out of your comfort zone and take responsibility for your life. Peers can have a positive and negative influence on us at an early age; we need folks that encourage, cheer us on and motivate us to do well. Our elders, our parents, our coaches, our teachers and even our bosses have that capability. Today we're faced with too much negativity and just too much competition. We can't just be happy. We have to be jealous. We have to be mean, we have to be envious and most importantly we have to post it on social media. Ownership means, I will take full responsibility of my life.

Bob Cappel, in his white apron, I am sure was the hit of the town. Why? He had a job at a young age, he was developing social skills beyond his years, further than what he envisioned social skills to be. In

1965, at the young age of 18, he was mounting personal positive habits that would modify him into a businessman down the road. What I find interesting in writing this is that today getting a job as a teenager seems more of a hassle and is looked on as more of a negative skill that it did in its heyday.

Bob had money. $$$$$$$$$$$$$$$$$$$$$$ Once again, BOB HAD MONEY. Can teenagers say that today? I don't think so. Sure some do, but that means getting a job, and many, let's be honest, don't want to, because their parents allow them to sit on their rear-end. They want to play video games, they want to text, hangout on Instagram, play on the Internet, watch a cat play piano on YouTube, upload videos of themselves doing ridiculous stuff; twerking, eating powdered cinnamon as fast as they can or even sucking on a bottle to blow their lips up. What a waste of time! And people ask what is wrong with America today? Too much time on their hands. Or they are so "busy" watching horrible acts of violence on their phone and sharing it with their friends, that even if they had a job, they would be fired. Their parents would be outraged as to why their child was fired. The reason is, there is no "ownership" and parents are the root cause of that problem. Boy is this a massive problem today.

Parenting

What Bob had that we need revived, is we need to come to the front burner as parents who encourage children to balance their lives. Not to be one dimensional, but dabble in a few good things here and there. I know the 1960's had its issues; Vietnam, the civil rights movement, Kennedy assassination, Martin Luther King assassination and a plethora of other nationwide issues. But, Bob's parents made sure he was occupied on building his foundation, building a future for their son. Giving him the leadership skills he needed, the morals he needed to be successful in life and the strict accountability of his parents rules. Communicating with Bob on his whereabouts, knowing his son's friend's, knowing their son's friends parents, knowing Bob's teachers, coaches, and the list goes on and on.

Personal ownership is running very thin these days and we blame everything on others. Taking no responsibility for ourselves. Back then you had to. You had to get up and dust yourself off if you wanted to make it in life. There were no freebies in life and let's be honest, it builds true character having a job as a teenager. Bob was right there in thick of it. The brush was so thick he could use a machete to cut it.

Strategy

Ownership of one's life is how we separate the doers from the wishers. I know Bob wished he could be a millionaire at age 18, but that wouldn't have been a grand beginning to Bob's young career. A handout would have crushed Bob. Bob was a tactical person, he planned out his weeks, his summer months, his work schedule and his personal life very well. But what Bob captured in those early days at the grocery story were developmental concepts that would carry him through his whole adult life and even today.

Brown bags, no plastic. You did not have a choice. Milk in glass jugs, meat wrapped in wax coded paper with a string or tape. Cash registers did not calculate the price, nor did they automatically calculate the customers change. You had to count in your head, you had to do "math". Skills acquired working at a store were so valuable; community skills, communication skills, planning ahead, watching the weather, forecasting future needs based on holidays. First communions, graduations, Christmas, Easter, Mother's Day, Father's Day, Fourth of July.

Bob was present; walking, running, scouring all over the store. Getting this prepared, ordering that and he was not even twenty years old. He had added responsibility that some will never comprehend, but Bob cherished it. Bob appreciated it. Bob was so immersed into his job that effort was not work, it was a game. Calling people on the phone, placing orders, unloading the supply truck, washing the windows, placing the weekly ads in the windows and carrying groceries out to the customer's car. Bob would listen to the radio while on the job; no head phones. Buffalo Springfield, Lou Reed, 700 WLW (Reds game) all in the background, while he was sweeping and mopping. He had no stations to select, no skip, just a am/fm radio. He was content with that. For the radio was just background noise. Customers came first; others placed first, himself second. Not knowing what putting himself first even meant.

Bob was still a teenager. He still had Dan and all of buddies. He still went out on dates, he still went to drive-in movies. He went to Reds games with his dad, Herb, to watch Ted Kluszewski compete. He was still a young man balancing his life. It was not all work, nor was it all play. Bob, through the guidance of his mom and dad, understood you have to have fun, both at work and outside of work.

MENTOR

The ownership of Bob's life was truly touched by Bernie, the owner of the grocery. Bernie believed in him as well as his own son, Dan. Bob saw him as a father figure, and trusted him with his decisions on giving Bob more responsibility. Responsibility that would take him from ground zero to the pinnacle in due time.

But ownership is more than just taking responsibly for one's life. It's gaining new knowledge, gaining new perspectives on new invaluable traits that will carry you from one level to the next. Bernie was right there. Today we laugh when kids get their drivers license at 16, complaining it's way too early. We set the bar to twenty-one on the drinking age, stating young adults just aren't trusty worthy enough. Yet, at 18 they can sign up and go defend our country, but they are too young to drink. The teenager can join the armed services and can take the wheel on a million dollar Hummer, or a 50 caliber machine gun, or an unmanned drone over Afghanistan. Bernie furnished Bob with the tools to take his life by the horns. Through the guidance of his first manager. Bob was given a tremendous apparatus to establish his niche in the business world.

LEARNING

At eighteen we really don't have the concept of what we are going to do. Yet, we have a inspiration. Those dreams start to shrink down some, being a pro ball player at 18 has come and gone. If your aren't playing anymore, then it's gone. Playing in a rock band? Well if you aren't playing anymore those pipe dreams are gone. They can come back, but they have been moved to the back burner.

Through his parents, Bob had to act on what was relevant vs. what was irrelevant. So once again after graduating from McNicholas high school in 1967, Bob enrolled into what is called Cincinnati State today, or Cincinnati Technical College back then. Bob enrolled into a sales marketing program, which led him to earning an associate's degree.

Bob had his priorities straight. He placed school first and work second, but he never left the butcher business. He continued working at Hornschemeier Grocery on the weekends, while balancing school on the other side. Bob was not just a student, and I want to make that clear. He had a part-time job and went to school at the same time. He was not one dimensional. Bob was still getting in his passion on the back end. His love of work. Bob knew though, that he had to get a college degree and an associate's degree was a superb fit.

Motivation

It's April 22, 2015 as I write this. Just yesterday at the Indianapolis Airport I had to interview a slew of young men and women. In order to get a job at the airport, you must have a high school diploma or a G.E.D. The minimum. Here it is 2015 and a G.E.D is the minimum, but back in 1967, Bob was pushing himself to accomplish more. He was off to college, off to make an enhanced future. Today though, people say it is tough to go to school and work. I say if Bob can do it, so can you. There is no difference between the 60's and 2015. It just takes ownership of one's life. Today we have the same role models and parents who encourage their kids as they did in the 60's. The problem is no one wants to take the lead. No one wants to push kids. No one wants to challenge them to do more. We may hurt their feelings. Boo hoo. Suck it up and get going. Motivation is a choice, yet, when we see others who are motivated to do well, such as Bernie, that artery bleeds over to others, as it did to Bob.

Coaching

Bob saw Bernie as a beacon, as a leader in a industry that takes effort, is part of the community, and is a part of molding future leaders. Bob saw this glow in Bernie's store. Bob loved the notion of the grocery so well he studied in marketing. The understanding of why people buy items, why people return to shop at the same store over and over, and the buying routine. He was developing knowledge on the theme that would accommodate him soundly in his near future, but he had no suspicion. He was laying tracks, yet his final destination was nowhere to be seen. Bob took it upon himself to procure outside skills that would assemble the framework on top of the foundation he had already created.

Bob was taking possession of his life through his own actions. He did not drop out of school. I am sure he thought about it. It's harsh, the professors are too hard, they don't appreciate students, too far to drive, no where to park, it's raining out, the hills in Cincinnati are terrible and it's snowing. Many would have skipped this day. Which leads to skipping weeks and dropping out completely. Bob had the ethics of a strong willed individual all because he had parents and managers who encouraged him to further his education.

Root.........Root..............Root; for the home team. For if they don't win it's a shame.

Lessons

The take me out to the ball game lyrics can shed light on what we must perform today, as we have finished in years past. Parents rooted and cheered us on. They pushed us to read more, go outside and play. Cutting your knee open was not a crisis. Getting a little sunburn was not the death of us. Drinking out of a hose was not seen as instant death. Elders were interested in what we were doing, engrossed in talking with complete strangers. They told us you will get your driver's license, you will get a summer job and you will volunteer. It was just a little push to achieve more. It was just the correct way. Parents and teachers were more than just elders, they were the force behind getting us to be more in-tuned as to what the future requires. Ashamed! Parent's are let down here and there. We will make bad choices as teenagers. I know Bob made a few as does everyone. But, we learn from our mistakes and we move on. We don't lose sight of the ball. We get back in the game and hammer down and focus our efforts. We keep our head down, eye on the ball, back elbow up and we crush the ball. We never lose sight of the big picture. We complete the game. We never stop and say this is too hard. We know we must finish. Bob's parents were the biggest fan section he ever had. They loved him, guided him, and held him accountable for his actions. What did Bob do? He earned his diploma.

CHAPTER 4 THE BEGINNING

VISION

L anding your first so called "real Job" is a bunch of malarkey. Every job is an authentic job; you are either all in or all out. You can't be 50/50. If that is the case, then it's time to abandon ship. Or it will sink itself. While attending Cincinnati Technical School, Bob was fortunate enough to land a co-op job in the dental supply field. Yes, an apprentice for a few years in the grocery industry, Bob now found himself tackling a whole new world. The art and craft of selling, marketing, phone conversations and meeting new people in the white collar world. Bob was just twenty years old and the year was 1969. The same year we landed on the moon. It's funny that a dream and a vision are talked about all the time and how one builds on another. President Kennedy was assassinated in 1963, yet before he was killed, he proposed the concept of landing on the moon. His dream of witnessing this was taken on November 22, 1963. Yet, on July 20, 1969 his vision came alive. What Kennedy did was lay the core structure of developing the means of getting to the moon and his vision is what got us there. He saw in color, while others saw in black and white. He saw the picture long before it came to fruition and that is what leaders do. They see the potential long before others, and they reach out and challenge others through guidance and nurturing.

DEVELOP

In this case, Bernie witnessed the vision in Bob. He observed the young man's drive and his core attributes flourishing and he took it upon himself to reach out to Bob and present him a full time managerial position. So in 1970, after dabbling around in the medical field, and earning his two year degree, Bob landed his first key role. A stance that would forever change his life. It was a duty that Bernie had seen for years. Bernie detected in Bob the future endeavors Bob could not predict. From the independent leagues to Single A, Bob moved up. From the developmental leagues, to one with accountability and the mental attributes to prosper, Bob moved up. Bob knew he was excellent, but to be great, others have to rally around you and through proper reinforcements, offer you the initial chance to shine. That is what Bernie did. Bernie allowed Bob to take on a mission that was far different than stocking shelves, far different than mopping the floors. It was a leadership role, a player-manager position that allows one to work alongside his peers and still have the working knowledge to govern the store.

For three years Bob assisted Bernie running the store. Learning more than what it takes to be a stock boy. Now, Bob was learning the key ingredients of a butcher, and learning leadership characteristics that would carry him even further. Bob was now knee deep in the process of the store, understanding how to prepare sausage; fresh sausage, cured cooked sausages, cured dry sausages; understanding key words such as sodium, potassium nitrate and nitrate. He had to understand how temperature plays a key role. Each case was different than the other to keep products fresh.

Bob's understanding of the basics was now beginning to payoff, his understanding of knives; butcher knife, 10 inch, 6 inch beef skinner, 5 inch narrow boning, 6 inch curved blade boning knife and a 6 inch wide blade boning knife were seen as a paint brush. His artistic side was gleaming at the store. For Bob understood beyond the basics at twenty. He understood the reason for a bone ax, he knew how to handle a 25 inch bone saw and the reason for a heavy duty meat cleaver. For at twenty, Bob was well past the fundamental understanding of what a butcher is.

Bob was no longer the newbie in a industry that was thriving in Cincinnati, where the local butcher was still needed. They were still seen as the experts long before the Walmart or even super Kroger. The community shopped at stores, but when your needs included deli meat, fresh ground beef or steak, they would visit the butcher. Cincinnati, having a long tradition for excellent food, due to its German heritage, was a superb place for Bob to learn from Bernie. Goetta, not just any sausage, a German sausage was in demand. So you had to know more than the basics to survive a highly populated German city such as Cincy. You had to know your brats and metts, as well as the other fifty cuts of meat, and where they originated from.

Bob's background served him well. The two years leading up to college at Hornschemeier Grocery served him so well that Bob now understood beyond the basics of a butcher shop. Bob knew how to take care of the tabletop meat slicers, he knew how to clean and handle the grinders. Bob knew how to handle the demands of the customer's needs, he knew thin sliced or thick sliced. He understood the customer's needs.

Understand

The word butcher comes from the word "boucher," meaning "slaughter of goats." The butcher was to slaughter the animal right away, break it down into edible parts and sell it to the customer, who would take it and cook it up that day. Bob, "the butcher".... It has a great ring to it, but Bob now was understanding the roll he had earned, not taking any of it for granted. Through Bernie, Bob knew more than what a flank was, knew more than what a tenderloin was. Bob was understanding the flow of a superb butcher shop. He was grasping what foods were in demand and how to prepare food instead of just cutting it up. Bob was becoming a connoisseur in the field, the go-to-guy at Hornschmeier Grocery. Bob knew that a Cowboy steak is called a rib-eye, he knew that by keeping the filet and the strip together it was called a T-bone.

Bob's working knowledge was radiating. He was moving up and down behind the counter as if Michelangelo was working the Sistine chapel. Bob knew what take a number meant, well before Ickey Woods made it famous on a tv commercial. Bob knew that lines were forming and Bob knew how to get them in and out with a smile. People were buying quality substance at a rapid and orderly pace. He knew how to prepare ahead of time, meet the days demands, and close down the grocery. Never taking his job as just a butcher for granted. He was growing into a master butcher, but there is more to a store than beef and customers.

Bob understood sanitation and working with blood and guts can get a little creepy. Plus spoiled meat can cause bacteria infested food. Bob was learning the regulations of the USDA; understanding the diseases caused by spoiled meat; tuberculosis, brucellosis, listeriosos, teaniasis, trichinois, and a slew of others. Bob was taking temperatures of coolers, self auditing the store, handling board of health audits, handling surprise inspections, handling paper work trails, fixing broken equipment, handling lighting and of course handling customers that had an issue. Bob was just twenty years old and he was in command of the store, under Bernie's tutelage. Bernie was giving Bob more and more responsibility and Bob was soaking it all in like sponge.

Sʏsᴛᴇᴍ

Today we would say that is way too much for a twenty-one year old. Then again we also say that having a forty hour job for a forty year old is way too much. The work ethic today is just as prominent as it was back in the 70's. The only thing is, people just don't want to work hard. They want entitlements. They want to be given the title without the effort. They want instant gratification without even sweating or drudging through it. The end product is what we hunger, but we don't want to do the passage, yet the trek is the best part. Do you want your kids to be a teacher? Well, they better get their master's degree. Want them to be commercial pilot? Better get them to Ohio State and study aviation, then go off to the military, fly for four years then maybe, just maybe, they will have a chance to get up in the clouds. Nothing is free anymore. Fake it until you make it is long gone for the many.

ACTION

We all want the gigantic contract, the big deal. But what Bob is doing right now in the book at twenty-one is what staff do at age forty-five. He is in control of a store. He is the assistant manager overseeing a few employees, yet, he is rolling up his sleeves and getting things done alongside them. He is preparing himself for tomorrow by working his butt off today. The end product, truly is never done; we tweak it a little bit more each year to make us stronger, gain more wisdom, gain more insight, gain new perspectives, and we are never satisfied with where we are. Yes, we are happy to be at this level, but we want to go higher. For the further you want to get the fewer and fewer people are there. The doers keep plugging along and those that are average just stop. They are satisfied with where they are. Average is boring anyway. It's harder to be amazing and each day making the best of it. Bob was doing that in 1971-1973 under Bernie. Bob was giving more each day, striving to be the best he could at the level he was. Taking money to the bank, closing up the store, cleaning up the floor, doing the daily paper work and having a blast while doing it. Each day Bob knew that he would reach the top of the mountain he was climbing. What was at the top was yet to be seen, but his dreams and visions were alive and well. He had a promising future, but it was up to him. New doors will open and old ones will close soon, but it was up to Bob to jump or fall off. He chose to jump and go for it.

CHAPTER 5 AGE OF EXPLORATION

We all love comfort; fireplaces, grandma's house, throw blankets. We love keeping it simple, we love painless, we love structure, we love hot showers, we love snow on Christmas eve, and we love getting birthday cards. When it comes to the business world, we love having the same manager, whether they are trouble-free or harsh; we just know how to work with them. We know the ins and outs, what time they get there, what days they work, how they like paper work filed, days meetings are going to transpire. We, are in a comfort zone with them. We know where they will park, when their kids games are, why they show up late to work and so on and so on. Yet, we as employees are in the same world as they are. We know we're going to hear about Martha's weekend again. We're going to hear about Steve's parents illness, again. We know we are going to get yelled at by Wendy for not refilling the candy dish on her desk. We know the whole time slot, as if we're on a reconnaissance mission. Gathering up all the simple details as if we are planning an invasion of some sort.

Variety

As an adult we can look beyond the mundane. We can focus on our work and push through the dreadful days, making the best of it. But as a young adult right out of college, we need to face more missions, we need to experience more. We cannot get comfortable on the job, we have to learn from others, we have to experience more trials and tribulations. We have to climb and climb up the ladder; seeing more, enduring more. Working with others, both of different race and religion, of different backgrounds, of different ages, different gender, different everything. This is what Bob is about to do. He's about to jump ship.

Bob was to go from Double A ball to Triple A; he was going to move up based on the very store that made him, was closing down. In 1973, after three years as manager of Hornschemeier Grocery, Bernie decided it was time to close the store down. The 70's was a time for the suburbs to explode, sons and daughters were no longer moving into the same neighborhoods as their parents, they were moving out and pushing further and further away from downtown. Bernie had seen this coming, and before he took it on the chin, he took upon himself to see a future that was bright instead of future that was cloudy and uncertain. So at the young age of 24, Bob was leaving his comfort zone for the first time, but still in the same game. Bob went to a different team.

Talent

When you are in niche business, as is the deli or butcher business, people know you. They've heard of you, and when you are great; they want you. Bob headed right over to another butcher shop in the same area of town, Mt. Washington. This time landing a job at Hitches Meats, and now out of his comfort zone. Bob's skills were now radiant; they were gleaming and he knew he made a solid move.

Unique

Wanting more in life seems to be the American way anymore, we want more substance. Objects will not get you to where you want to go, items are just that, something tangible that gives us instant gratification. We love having them, we love sharing them with others, we flaunt them, we have them and mine is better. I own them and you don't. Look what I have and you don't. Keeping up with the Joneses and the

Smiths is just flat out a waste of time. Try keeping up with Cappel, Bob Cappel. The year is 1973. I was two years old as Bob was transitioning from one store to another. Here he is a stellar young man; good looking, hard driven, college graduate taking the fearful leap from the known to the unknown. Sure, the same butcher atmosphere awaits him, the knives look the same, the salami tastes the same and the ground beef still comes from the same source as Hornschemeier Grocery did. Bob was a newbie at a new location. Bob's background landed him the job, and his previous mentor Bernie guided him up to this point of his career. Bob, though, had to move forward and separate himself from the grocery business and redirect his energy into a full time butcher shop. A butcher shop is way different than a grocery store. Now you are in the elements of the beef industry. You are clearly in a niche business, a precious business that "ALL" know well and good create happy Saturday backyard cookouts and create scrumptious deli trays for Christmas time. Steaks furnished with precision so well, you could taste the end product before walking out the door.

SKILLS

Bob leaped from one endeavor to the next without feeling sorry for himself. He had to get a job after Hornschemeier's closed down. He knew that the butcher shop was going to guide him down a path of future greatness, but Bob made the choice to land a job quickly. He did not hesitate. He did not drown in his sorrows and he didn't say "I'll take the next 6 months off." Bob took his skills from running a grocery to Hitches Meats. Bob got the job because Bob wanted the job. That itself is why Bob is doing well. Bob took ownership of his life and was not looking back. Bob was creating his future. He was going to do it by landing in a industry that was still seen as alive and well; the local butcher shop.

Learning a trade is seen today by some as below our standards, it is seen as still blue collar. It is seen as you are not worthy of anything else except to do physical labor. Well I tell you what, as I write this, I wrote a check yesterday to the local plumber for $228 dollars. For two hours of work. If he does 5 jobs a day that is $1,140 dollars in a day. $1,140 X 5 days = $5,700 dollars in a week. $5,700 X 4 weeks = $22,800. $22,800 X 12 months = $273,600 dollars a year. Okay, are you laughing now?????????

The local butcher then as it is now, is seen as an expert in the artistic world of culinary arts. The Food Network is booming; cooking magazines, cooking books, Grilling for Dummies, man size grills are no longer for just men, women grill and believe me my wife is better than I am. We want good quality meat, we want good quality cheese, we want fresh veggies, fresh fruit, organic this and that, with a straight from the farm environment. What Bob was doing was creating a demand for expertise, at the young age of twenty-four. Most kids today still live at home at twenty-four, some kids are still working on their degrees at twenty-four and still don't have a job. They are waiting for the correct moment to come, to land in their lap. Swoop them up and take them to their ultimate job. Boom, you are CEO. Way to go.

IMPROVEMENT

Bernie, created and molded Bob into understanding in order to get to where he was, you must endure and challenge yourself to achieve more. Don't sit on the side lines. Be in the game of life. Bob was all in. At Hitches Meats, Bob was learning the art and craft of being a first rate butcher. He was honing the skills, knowledge and lingo of the industry. He now was learning the key parts of the cow. Chuck, rib, short loin, sirloin, round, tenderloin, top sirloin, bottom sirloin, brisket, navel, shank, flank. He was ripping into a pig, knowing what the parts of the pig created. Neck chops, shoulder, loin chops, fat back, jowl bacon, bacon, ribs and of course ham. But it did not stop there. He was now preparing turkeys for Thanksgiving and Christmas. This young man at twenty-four understood the filet breast, chicken tenders, leg drum stick, leg and thigh. Bob was not standing around, he was getting into his job full force. At twenty-four, Bob was growing into a culinary authority. The 10,000 hours theory was starting to take shape. Each week improving, each week gathering more concepts, each week understanding the wants and needs of the store owner and how to provide top quality meat to the clientele. Bob was working alongside gentleman who took an inkling as to Bob's passion for being a butcher. He was becoming more and more tuned into what his future was looking like. Yet at twenty-four, do we really know what our future has in store? No we don't, yet when you enjoy your job and have a passion for it, the light is a little brighter. Bob could see doors opening at every turn. He had a gift. He had a calling. It just was over the horizon, but what was it?

Being an expert in one's field is a superb accomplishment, but what does being an expert really mean? Do we stop growing and just share our love with others? Do we stop and gaze at our past, and say, "look what I have done to get here." In 1976, at the age of now twenty-seven, Bob was going to take what he had learned over to yet another butcher shop. Moving ever so closer to downtown Cincinnati, forging his way to the roots of the city. Placing himself now in a well established butcher shop, one that had been around for years. Mr. Cappel was growing again, his expertise at Bernie's store and Hitches Meats were building up to another move, another move that would allow him to grow and start to mature in the meat business.

INCREASE

This time with three years under his belt as a butcher, and four years working at a grocery store, Bob was getting a handle on what his calling was. The problem was where was this road leading him? Where was this going to get him? He knew he could not keep leaving a structure every three years, that wouldn't build a career. He knew something was ahead. So Bob, being a go-getter, not waiting on others to push him, pursued another butcher shop. This time Huber Meats in east Hyde Park. A well established shop, one that had been around for years, where Bob would learn the demands of new clients and consumers. But he would not last long at all here (6 months). For he was now about to hear the calling that others had foreseen years ago. He was about to take a leap of confidence. A leap that had fear, concerns, and a ton of mystery to it. A leap so life-size that those close to him encouraged him, but others would question him.

"He who works his land will have abundant food."- Proverbs 12:11

CHAPTER 6 10,000 HOURS PAYS OFF

AUTHORITY

Bob was just like any other entrepreneur, he knew all along he was first-rate and that his work ethic would pay off. So here it was 1976 at the age of twenty-seven having had a past that most businessmen have when they reached forty. A keen eye on a niche business and Bob was ready to get caught off guard.

10,000 hours. As I noted in the preface, the authors said that 10,000 hours in a constant routine builds and leads into being an expert in that designated field. In Bob's case I will break it down.

Hornschemeier Meats
1965-1967 Part time. 20 hours a week x 52 weeks = 1040 hours. 1040 x 2 years = 2080 hours.
Full time in the summer, another 20 hours x 9 weeks x 2 years = 360 hours.
1967-1969 Part time. 20 hours a week x 52 weeks = 1040 hours.

1040 x 2 years = 2080 hours.
1970-1973 Full time. 40 hours a week x 52 weeks = 2080 hours.
2080 x 3 years = 6240 hours.

In just the grocery business, Bob had a total of 10,730 hours. Expert at age twenty-four.

Hitches Meats
1973-1976 Full Time 40 hours a week x 52 weeks = 2,080 hours. 2,080 x 3 years = 6,240 hours.

Huber Meats
1976 Full Time 40 hours a week x 26 weeks = 1,040 hours

In just the butcher business, Bob had collected 7,280 hours. Off by 2,720 hours for being called expert.

SUPPORT
At the young age of twenty-seven Bob had 17,680 hours of practice. That is vast, considering he is not even the age of thirty. What Bob had done back in 1976 is seen today as a workaholic. I know Bob could collect social security at the age of twenty-five for the amount of taxes he had already paid into the system. Was Bob really working above and beyond the standards of an employee? I say NO! Bob was driven and thriving with a passion and a calling of being a butcher. What Bob had is direction and guidance from others. He had Bernie and his father; two key role models.

Having a job is the American way, sitting back and excepting handouts and freebies is just hard for me to comprehend. Bob was not waiting, he was going for it. Bob, at twenty-seven, was about to get the conversation of a life time. An occasion that he been groomed for.

FRIENDSHIP
We all take different paths on our journey. I mention Dan, Bernie's son and Bob's best friend. The two were running mates all through grade school, high school and even after graduation. Bob took one journey that I explained, but Dan took another path. Dan went to college

and got his degree in accounting. He then went off to the Navy for four years. After his stint he came back. Dan as well worked at Hornschemeier Grocery, but after college he branched off and created his own life. Still, through maintaining his friendship with Bob, they would still go out as buddies, go to games and cook outs, maintaining their strong friendship. Dan wore a white shirt and a red tie to work. Bob wore a white apron, stained from carcass residue. Dan knew the book keeping aspect of the business world and Bob knew the guts of the business world. Two totally different worlds, one was on his feet ten hours a day, the other was at a desk running numbers. One had a hour lunch break, one was grabbing a bite in-between customers. One sharpened pencils, one sharpened knives. One took two showers a day, one only took one. One was networking with customers over the phone, one was networking with consumers face to face.

The two were so opposite, yet they both had a enthusiasm for what they were doing. Both were people persons. They both enjoyed meeting new people, shaking hands and loved the art of vocation. Bernie shaped the two to reach out to others through proper customer service, through understanding the needs of customers and of course, trained them both on the responsibilities of running a business. He taught them in cooperation, which simultaneously their potential was growing as a team. The two, at eighteen, had no idea that they were being set up for one day as partners.

TEAM

In July of 1976, Dan and Bob had a conversation, one that would change their lives forever. The conversation of let's go into business together. The foreshadowing was pretty easy to see, but neither one of them really knew it at eighteen. They would create the concept of opening a butcher shop way out in the suburbs of Cincinnati. Young families were moving out to Anderson Twp. Young families with a need to push further away from the hustle and bustle of downtown. One where you could raise a family, have an excellent community and start out fresh with bigger homes and more breathing space. The timing was correct and the two would make that dream become factual.

"I fear not the man who has practiced 10,000 kicks once,but I fear the man who has practiced one kick 10,000 times."

Bruce Lee

CHAPTER 7 TIMING MAKES ALL THE DIFFERENCE

On July 3, 1962 a new sketch went into the works in Anderson Twp. The plans were permitted and construction would soon take place. The concept was to fabricate nine hundred homes on the north side of an eventful main artery, fifteen miles east of downtown Cincinnati. The two hundred and forty six acre community[4] was just north of Beechmont Avenue and would run on the east and west side of Eight Mile Road. The expenditure of the plans was in the seventeen million dollar range. It would have sufficient green space that a elementary school would be fashioned and with recreational fields as well. The development would be known as Summit Estates.

Investors state that timing is of the essence and timing is everything. We can wait and wait for the time to be right. However, there never really is a right time. You either jump in and thank yourself at a later date, or you wait and wait and wish you had started years ago. You start with the end in mind. You construct your own destiny and that is exactly what another young business man did in the early 70's. Earl Mette was his name, he saw the community layout and decided that he would jump right in and generate a little strip mall and anchor it with a convenient store. Earl was a visionary. He saw things long before others. He envisioned the nine hundred homes and saw $$$$$ figures with opportunities for growth. So much so, he had to erect a strip mall. Earl in retrospect formed a fresh Hornschemeier Grocery, one that Dan and Bob were working for only four miles away.

CHEER

Opening a business is frightening, it creates doubt. Will we do well? Will we make enough wealth to provide for our family? Is the timing right? Who do we market to? Who are our customers? Will customers be produced? Are we creating a need, creating a want? Are our skills fine enough to compete with others? What will people utter?

When we step out of our comfort zone, we are stepping into uncharted waters. We are stepping out of our inner circle and stepping into a whole new concept. We are taking a leap of faith because we are prepared. We are confident that we will do sound, knowing that what got us here will take us into our new roles. We don't listen to the lawnmowers. The very people who cut us down on our decision. They are just naysayers anyways. We surround ourselves with cheerleaders, ones who root us on and keep us energized.

OPPORTUNITY

In July of 1976, Bob and Dan would come together and create a bond in the business world. This time the two finally got the call up to the big leagues. A moment they had been waiting for, for years. Well, at least that is what Bernie and Herbert knew. They had a vision of opening their own butcher shop. Dan, with his wife and children, were living in the nine hundred home community. Dan saw the opportunity and jumped all over it. With Bob, the two would seize the moment and capture the suburb craze. With money saved, Bob took out a loan as well as Dan. They made contact with Earl at the convenient store and proposed the concept of opening a butcher shop. Earl, a superb business man took the notion and leased out a fraction of the strip mall to the young men.

For three months the two men gave up their jobs, put their future in each other's hands and started to construct a business. A business that Bernie and Herbert saw in them both years ago. At the young age of twenty-seven, the two entrepreneurs were off to the races. They had to start from scratch and build on a new endeavor.

CHAPTER 8 THE CLOCK RESETS

PLANNING

After three months of preparation, hundreds of hours of planning the store final took shape. On October 1st, 1976 Summit Meats opened its doors. This time the clock had to reset, the 10,000 hour rule got Bob to here. Now the 10,000 hour clock of ownership was at zero. Yes, the years of service building up to this day constructed a solid house, but now, this was a new house. Identical resemblance as the other stores Bob worked at, but this time Bob was in charge. Bob and Dan now were making decisions for themselves, making decisions for their future. Making decisions for their families.

The ladder was continuing to create steps, continuing to create more height for Bob. Marshall Goldsmith, one of my favorite authors, had a great title for his book. What Got You Here, Won't Get You There. The book was on how successful people become even more successful. The image on the cover was of a man climbing a ladder, which lead to another ladder. It sets the stage for we can go as high as we want. But we have to do extra to continue up the ladder of success. We must bestow superfluous sweat, as well as, study more in order for us to continue on our next journey. We have to step out of our comfort zone, and that is exactly what Bob and Dan did. The duo knew they were excellent, really brilliant in their occupations. So advanced, they wanted to share their passion with others. Share their desire and knowledge with the neighboring community.

Inc.com ran an article written by Darren Dahl. The title was, 10 reasons to run your own business.

Based on a survey of 462 small business owners, Darren collected the top 10 reasons 600,000 new businesses are created each year.

- You control your own destiny.
- You can find your own work/life balance.
- You choose the people you work with.
- You take on the risk and reap the rewards.
- You can challenge yourself.
- You can follow your passion.
- You get things done, faster.
- You can connect with your clients.
- You can give back to your community.
- You feel the pride in building something of your own.[5]

Emotions

Now to counter that theme, Bob and Dan had apprehension like they never had known before. Fear of the unknown, fear of failure, fear of rejection, fear of what will people articulate if they closed down or didn't make it. Fear..Who isn't scared of unexplored waters? We all are, but we must prevail over our fears and believe in what we are doing by having self-confidence in our operation. That is what Bob and Dan were doing. We are all terrified of something, but listen to your inner self. If it's worth pursuing and you believe in yourself, then do it.

In an article by Entrepreneur, written by Te-Erika Patterson. She writes on 10 fears you must overcome when starting a business.

- Not knowing where to start.
- Not being an expert.

- Being considered crazy.
- Not finding funding.
- Not being believed in.
- Not attracting customers.
- Being incapable of handling success.
- Failing the family.
- Not earning enough to recover the investment.
- Discovering everything goes wrong.[6]

My parents were born and raised in Cincinnati; my mom and dad both lived in Anderson Twp. Mom studied at Anderson high school, my dad, McNicholas high school. They were wed in 1969, and I was born in 1971. With my dad being in business he was transferred to Columbus, Indiana where my brother was born in 1972. From there, on to Louisville, Kentucky. Then in 1977 at the age of six my parents moved back to Cincinnati. This time moving into the subdivision of Summit Estates. We moved in on the east side of Eight Mile, the second stage of the development onto Muskegon. The residence was situated on the last path built in the neighborhood with a huge wooded area behind our residence. I would enter first grade upon moving back. An awe-inspiring dwelling to say the least. Four bedroom, two car garage, two story with a basement and a little under half an acre plot.

Together

The clock now was reset on Bob's foundation. He was now into his first year with his buddy, Dan. Taking all the small steps in his life and building a retail is not effortless. It's fun and exciting. The unknown territories being searched, the new store, new coolers, new chopping blocks. The new knives, new customers, new store hours. Bob and Dan remind me of two icons; Roy Disney and Walt Disney. Two pioneering individuals. Two brothers who built an empire because both were diverse. Walt had the vision and Roy had the skills. Together they were relentless. But these two we have heard of. Bob and Dan? Well, no. Bob and Dan are no different than Roy or Walt; they practiced the identical virtues, practice the matching skill set, rehearsed for years for center stage. They both had good stamina, excellent people skills and excellent work habits. Mutually the men knew that there is more to a store than loading shelves with tangibles. More to a store than just flipping the sign to "we are open". Both men had seen the calling many years ago. This time at the young age of twenty-seven, we feel we are too young, too immature. Yet, as you will witness there is no "right time". The moment was now and the time was right as long as you believe in what you are doing. They did.

A small business environment is more than selling hamburger, sausage links and chicken breasts. It's placing special orders for customers. It's listening to customers' needs, educating customers on the products. It's patience, it's excellent communication, it's connecting with the local community. It's staying open an extra half hour for a rush, it's opening early for a client that has a First Communion celebration with the family and the order is ready for pickup. Bob worked tirelessly, he brought his "A" game the minute the store opened. He worked six days a week, from open to close. The store was closed on Sundays, but you could find Bob scrubbing down the floor, conducting a deep clean. Sanitizing the store thoroughly. Yes, Bob understood money was tight, for it was his and Dan's investment. Together they both understood sacrifice, understood what teamwork meant, understood that in order to be successful, you have to do more. Bob knew one day his efforts would pay off, he knew his personality that Herbert, Marie and Bernie had taught him would be a asset toward his personal endeavors.

Bob's store was booooooooming, it was more than he could have ever dreamed up. However, the right location is only half the battle, the rest is up to the individual. Gaze at all the strip malls in key locations, yet, look at all the vacancy. It's more than looking out the window and wanting customers, it's being proactive. It also helps when the anchor store of the mall is flourishing (Convenient Food Mart). The anchor store was right next door in Bob's case. That is the very store that my mom and dad would drive down on the way to work and get gas, cigarettes', or cigars as in my dad's case. They would get a fresh cup of coffee and fill up the car as well. On weekends my parents would be there to get chips, beer, soda and all the other items they appropriately forgot, or ran out of in the middle of the family get together. When you are down there for the first time, you see a butcher shop is located right next door and there is a line at the counter. Not a big line but two or three people deep. You see behind the counter two men and their staff hustling around, yelling numbers. "Number 31, Number 32". You see firsthand a smile on their face, a swift step in their stride, a sense of humor, a good morning is hollered your way, a good afternoon, or hello Mrs. McManus. Hello Mr. Zimmerman. Hello Mrs. Schwartz. You knew that the butcher shop was not just about taking orders, the shop was about putting people first, taking care of the customer, by conducting business accordingly and showcasing the store in a very positive manner. Bernie taught Bob and Dan the essentials of business; give the customer so much more than a product, give them a reason to come back. Create a loyal customer. Once you do that, they will tell their friends.

CONNECTING

Bob's clock was reset. The 10,000 hour principle was just the beginning. But Bob knew he had to do more than take orders, now Bob had to go see firsthand where his meat was coming from. Bob told me he would go and visit slaughter houses in downtown Cincinnati; see firsthand the conditions in which his meat was being prepared and where his store received his shipment from. Bob was paying attention to the minute tasks that all owners had to deal with in order to understand the business in which they are in. Bob would visit Findlay Market in downtown Cincinnati, he would visually inspect the meat first hand. Bob was connecting with his vendors, then relaying that information to the customers. Bob would house 8,000 pounds of meat a week, or roughly 416,000 pounds a year at Summit Meats. Bob would visit distribution sites, such as HMI on the north side of Cincinnati. He would visit Kluener packing downtown on Massachusetts Avenue. Bob was educating himself, then turning around and delivering quality communication to his customers. Bob would visit Juergling in Camp Washington to see as well where his sides of beef would come from.

RESEARCH

What I find interesting about this, is Bob was not sitting on the side lines hoping to be engaged with his business. Bob was betrothed with his business. But where does this all begin? Influence from others. Bernie and Herbert influenced Bob so much that he took it upon himself to do extra, to provide more and in order to flourish one must step outside of one's comfort zone. Who really wants to visit a slaughter house? Who really wants to know where the beef comes from as long as its sanitary? I'll tell you who, "BOB", the store owner. His efforts as well as Dan's were creating a solid business, creating a butcher shop worth noting and worth visiting.

ALLOWED

Nine hundred homes in a new subdivision. Let's assume for this math problem that each house has two parents and three children. 900 x 5 = 4,500 possible customers. Needless to say that Summit Meats was growing and growing. Bob and Dan were not the only ones behind the core of the business, employees as well were taking shape. Bob's nephew Mike was onboard as well as a few ladies from the neighborhood and a few local high school kids. Bob and Dan could not do it all themselves, so yes, they had to delegate. As good leaders, they understood they had a ton of hats to wear, but they knew allowing others to grow, allowing others to take ownership of a small business as Bernie allowed them, would be key to their triumph.

CHAPTER 9 TAKING ON A NEW CONCEPT

In 1979 I was eight years old. I was going to school at Immaculate Heart of Mary. A good Catholic grade school on Beechmont Avenue. We had been living in our house for two years, and as a little guy I remember going down to Convenient Food Mart with my dad in his Nova. Sitting in the front seat with no seat belt. We would go down and get; Grippos chips and Mike Sells pretzels. The ones in the tin cans. We would stop by Summit Meats, and get burgers or lunch meat for the weekends and for my school lunches.

PROJECT

The good transaction that was going on in 1979 was that young adults were pushing further out from Cincinnati. They were moving out of Hamilton county and into Clermont county. Beechmont Avenue, or US 125 took you from Anderson Twp out east to Amelia. For cheaper taxes, you could get a bigger house for a cheaper price. More bang for your buck. Like two visionaries Bob and Dan thought it over and decided to try their hand at opening another store, placing Bobs nephew,

Mike as the store manager. The store was up and running, however it only lasted for eighteen months under their ownership. When opportunity knocks, you take it. The challenge was awesome. The new store was beautiful and their efforts were off the charts. They built a store up from the bottom and were thrilled to death on the three men's effort. However, an employee asked them both if they would be willing to sell the store, and with that approach, Bob and Dan took him up on it. The store was just doing average, so they were happy to get out from under it. They even set him up with monthly installments to finance the store.

DECISION

What is fun about being creative is that one door closes and another one opens, a vision is never really shut down. It just may have to be reshuffled to try another hand with the dealer. Failing in business is a huge fear. It's a huge investment that we never really recuperate from. What separates the good from the great is you get back up on that horse and go at it again. Bob and Dan knew their location was good there in Summit, so good that in 1980 they decided to go to Earl Mette (the landlord) with a concept that would take their business to new heights. Earl was expanding the strip mall and both men took it upon themselves to ask Earl if they could go to the end of the building instead of in the middle. Earl jumped to the occasion and with that, Summit Meats would occupy the small space as it is today. With that step came a new concept, a bakery.

CONCEPT

In 1981, Bob and Dan moved down to the south side of the building and came up with again another entrepreneurial concept. Let's open a bakery in the old space. Together they were now in the bakery business. Let's face it, what a grand concept. A butcher shop, convenience store, bakery and at the north end of the strip mall, a little bank. WOW!!!!! What a vision. Right place, right time. Four solid needs for a 900 home community. There would be no need to go up to the main street and shop. We can just be a one shop strip mall. Moms and dads can even walk up. A one minute drive or even ride a bike up.

However once again, a new business had to come to a stop. In 1983 Bob and Dan decided to close down the shop. Why? It was not because of lack of hard work, it was not due to lack of effort, it was because of dabbling with too many niche businesses. Fear, as you can tell, was not on Bob's and Dan's faces. They felt they could conquer anything and at the age of thirty-two they knew it was just time to close up shop. This time there was no buyer, however, Dan had connections to buyers in the bakery business. So they were able to recoup some of their initial investments.

ANALYSIS

A butcher shop is one thing, Bob's background had been built for that since 1965. A bakery was just too unfamiliar. Tons of early mornings, baking and preparing. Bob however was losing sight of what made him successful, what made him happy and what his strong point was. There is a great book called The Dip by Seth Godin. In it he speaks on why people quit a certain project, and why other projects keep going. His answer is straight and to the point; if you know it's not going well, you have put forth your best effort, then quitting a project is the best answer. Don't let it linger, persist year after year, cut your losses now and move on. Stand proud that you tried, for others never have. A balancing act is great for Ringling Brothers but not for a business owner that has zero back ground. You can have all the right players, yet, if your heart is telling you one thing, then follow it. Jack Palance's character said in the movie City Slickers, "Do you know what the secret to life is?" Billy Crystal's character said "No." Palace said, "It's one thing." Billy said, "What is that one thing?" Jack's answer was, "You have to find it."

"What is the point of being alive if you don't at lease try to do something Remarkable?"

John Green

CHAPTER 10 THE "ONE THING"

In 1984, I was thirteen years old, having had a few odd jobs in my life. I cut grass a little here and there. I shoveled snow in the neighborhood. I raked leaves for neighbors. Stacked firewood for neighbors and even delivered Avon products for a lady in our neighborhood on my bike. I played baseball all the time, plus soccer and basketball. My parents were involved in my life all the time. I have super parents and I love them to death. What is so memorable to me is riding my bike with my buddies down to the convenience store and getting candy bars, baseball cards or even an Icee. I knew Earl Mette, the landlord of the strip mall and the store owner of the convenience store. I knew Brad Kopf at the bank for that is where I opened up my first bank account and I knew of course Mr. Cappel. But I didn't know him that well. Let's face it at thirteen a butcher shop is not really where I wanted to hang out and visit.

In 1984, Bob Cappel found his "one thing", the one thing was owning the butcher shop all by himself. For eight years, Bob and Dan had worked side by side on creating a demand and a need for a thriving business. The concept of buying out his partner finally took shape and in that year, Bob became the sole proprietor of Summit Meats. It was the right time for Bob to take the leap and the dream of owning his own business on his own. Dan took him up on his offer, Bob took the lead role and began to forge his own butcher shop (still under the same name, Summit Meats).

OTHERS

Quick, name a famous butcher. Times up...What did you come up with? The first one that came to my mind was Sam from The Brady Bunch. The gentleman who dated Alice. What about Robert Leroy Parker, aka. Butch Cassidy. Yes, Butch Cassidy received his nickname from his period as a butcher in Rocksprings, Wyoming. While working on a dairy farm for Mike Cassidy, a cowboy and cattle rancher in his teenage years. Here's one for you. After high school Michael Hegstrand was a butcher, aka. the Hawk from WWF, The Road Warriors. One big name was Niccolò Machiavelli. His father, Bernardo was a butcher back in the 1500's in Florence, Italy. Niccolò went on to be Secretary of War, ambassador to France and wrote the book The Prince. As the movie title goes, What About Bob? Why is it that when we are young, elders say, grow up and do something with your life. Be somebody and do something immense. Yet, we search and search as if on an expedition or mining a cave. We keep searching as if there has to be something greater than what our parents have done or accomplished. That is a bunch of "BS." I truly know that to be successful in life is to be happy. Money can't buy that.

PERSPECTIVE

To tell someone you are a CEO is impressive. To tell someone you are a lawyer is impressive. To tell someone you are a news anchor is impressive. To tell someone you are a teacher is impressive. To tell someone you are a tennis player is impressive and to tell someone you are a butcher is impressive.

To share with someone that you own the butcher shop; now that is impressive. To build a company from the ground up with an outstanding partner, then ask to buy him out, takes guts. Bob and Dan were buddies. They were like peas and carrots. Their minds were garnished with positives that most people don't see today. The influence on the both of them from, Bernie to Herbert, to their families, to their customers. It was a classic scene out of a black and white movie. That stuff just does not happen. But it did. Bob knew his time had come to purchase the half and create a whole, to create his own store that had the elements of more challenges and more uphill battles; yet he was not going to turn and run with his tail between his legs. If that was the case, he would have done that after his second store was sold or the bakery closed. No, Bob was happy. Bob had the characteristics to be the sole owner of his own shop. Bob knew the business. Bob lived the business. Bob was joyful. He was content for no other reason than "HE" was making it happen. Bob found his "one thing." Giving his niche expertise to others, made him happy and customers loved him.

In a Forbes magazine article, written by Eric T. Wagner. He speaks on five reasons 8 out of 10 business fail:

- Not really in touch with customers through deep dialogue.
- No real differentiation in the market.
- Failure to communicate value propositions in clear, concise and compelling fashion.
- Leadership breakdown at the top.
- Inability to nail a profitable business model with proven revenue streams.[7]

So here we are, the year is still 1984 and Bob just bought out his business partner. Let's look at why 80% of business fail, but more closely, let's look at why 20% of the business succeed. I love the Pareto Principle; The 80/20 rule and this is why it always seems to work. In this case, let's just look at Bob.

1. Not in touch with customers. Bob had been groomed for this day since he was sixteen years old. Bernie had been educating him on how to put the customer first, how to fulfill the customer's needs and how to communicate with them.

2. No real differentiation. Summit Meats was surrounded by nine hundred homes. The doors opened in 1976 and for eight years custom-

ers have been coming up in droves because Summit Meats was a niche shop. No supermarket atmosphere, just Bob and his staff. They knew the customers names and what streets they lived on. Bob and my dad went to the same high school as well as others in the neighborhood. The human connection was present.

3. Failure to communicate. Wrong again. Bob's communication skills, organizational skills and planning skills were off the charts. Why? Once again Hornschemeier Grocery, Hitches Meats and Huber Meats all set him up for success. When you are sixteen and in the business of a niche market, you discover the skills necessary to thrive. Christmas, Thanksgiving and Fourth of July. Bulk orders. At thirty-five, Bob's soft skills were off the charts. He knew how to articulate with awareness and knew how to speak with familiarity to the customers.

4. Leadership breakdown. Crash and Burn. Those were not in Bob's dictionary. The words he used were overcome and adapt. To lead is easy. To have leaderships skills is another. Bob had both. Why? He had seen firsthand the success of three other businesses and he developed his own skill sets. Working 7 days a week. Scrubbing floors and cleaning coolers alongside others is leadership. Plus, getting staff to understand the outcome is essential to leadership. Staff want to work hard alongside you, because they respect you and enjoy working with you.

5. Inability to nail a profit. P&L statements are a must have in a successful business. But you must have more profit than loss in order to stay afloat. Let's face it; skating on thin ice is really stating you are about to tread water. The nine hundred homes were Bob's family. Mathematically, it was his for the taking. Bob, though had to present a quality product; a spotless store, welcoming staff and a clean cut image. Fake it till you make it. That was not Bob. He was authentic, plus always in high spirits all the time. Those traits generate a profit.

EXPERTISE

Summit Meats was Bob's store. It was now up to Bob to take it under his wing and continue to grow his passion even further. Trust. Big word back in the 80's as it is today. It seems we just can't trust anyone. We are afraid that we are being misled, misguided or even misinformed. Bob was trustworthy and customers respected him. Oh, I am sure some customers did not like a few things about his shop; little higher than the supermarket, Bob did not carry soda, or Bob was not open till 9pm. But the many outweigh the few. You can't accommodate all the customer's needs. Cheese from Switzerland was tough to carry. Not enough demand. I am sure certain types of deli meats Bob could not carry due to spoiling too quickly. Just not an ample demand.

COACHING

Bob now was on his own, he had his nephew Mike alongside him behind the counter. He had Karen and he started to even hire local high school kids and develop them. As I interviewed Bob, he was hesitant on this answer of hiring high school kids. I know Bob got a lump in his throat, for what Bob was doing was creating another Bob and he now was Bernie. He paused. He was reflecting and he knew. Looking back it was the changing of the guard routine. He was the elder. Roles were changing. Maybe he never thought of it till now. Bob was influencing others as Bernie and his dad did to him. Bob now was the scholar and others were the pupil. He was the master and the young were the apprentice. What else took place with Bob owning his "OWN" business is how his family got involved. His wife Penny was now his book keeper. She was running the P&L statements and balancing the budget. She was at home working on the books, keeping tally of the cash flow, on the bills and keeping a keen eye over Bobs investment. Bobs job was the lead butcher, the master craftsman. Bob's wife was the new CPA without a license. She was a behind the scene partner, and like many say; "you can't do everything on your own."

CHIEF

Bob found his "One Thing." He found his passion, he found his calling. Yet, his path led him right to owning his own store. Sometimes the obvious is so clear that we just don't see it, we are looking to making a bigger impact on the world. Bigger does not mean better, better does not mean bigger. Small is the new big, and the butcher shop was just that. Expanding, stepping out of his niche had come and gone for Bob. His "One Thing", for the taking was right there. He was the owner of the business that he had made into a demand. Bob's craft took shape with the shop. Bob's characteristics got him here, and Bob's influence was taking shape on others.

"When I was 5 years old, my mother always told me that happiness was the key to life. When I went to school, they asked me what I wanted to be when I grew up. I wrote down 'happy'. They told me I didn't understand the assignment, and I told them they didn't understand life."

John Lennon

CHAPTER 11 TAKING YOUR PASSION TO THE CUSTOMER

In 1986, I was fifteen years old, and a freshman at McNicholas High School. I finally was in the "big time" or so I thought. I loved sports. I loved lifting weights. I loved my friends and I loved my coaches and teachers. I still had some odd jobs at that age without a drivers license. My mom would drop me off a one of her friends houses and I would work around their yard; rake leaves, pick up twigs, cut the grass, trim trees and prune a few braches. I was still helping out my mom's parents; Christmas lights, cleaning up the garage and so forth on the weekends. My mom and dad both influenced me to work hard, to save a few bucks, yet still find time for extracurricular activities. I went to dances, I went to school plays. I went to Coney Island on the weekends. I umpired baseball as well as, played summer ball. I was influenced by coaches such as Gary McKee, Skip Berger, Terry Zimmerman, Lou Schwartz, Kevin O'Brien, Pat Williams, and Phil Wilhoit. I had been influenced by teachers as well; Gary Pierson, Kay Horning and even my grade school principal Bob Ferrell. Principal Ferrell's detentions shaped me up a little and prepped me for high school. Neighbors helped influence me as well; Joe and Julie Ryan, John and Alice McManus. But what was missing was influence from a business stand point.

PROTECT

That same year, Bob was to take a step outside of his comfort zone and explore a fresh concept. He was to take his intensity to the customer. He was going to infiltrate the catering business. Now, opening a new butcher shop was sold off. Opening a new bakery store was closed down. This stride was to succeed. Why do we carry umbrellas? To protect ourselves from uncertain weather. Under that umbrella we protect what is sacred. We protect ourselves with everything we have. Summit Meats was precious (the store on Eight Mile road). The one at the corner of Clough and 8-Mile. The business was sacred and he was going to guard it with his life.

CUSTOMERS

Bob had everything he needed at his location, plus he already had a van. He had all the equipment he needed to march into a new world. This world though was more than food. It was about fulfilling people's needs and it's about having connections. Once again, nine hundred homes, three local high schools and a networking program that was off the charts took him to here. He knew it was time to expand. He didn't buy property, he didn't move the store and he didn't hire twenty new people. Bob new his limits. He knew catering would create another need and want for his customers. Influence works. It's a living breathing part of life. There are two kinds; positive and negative. With both, we learn. With both we excel and with both we can offer customers more.

STRUCTURE

We take what we have stumbled on and create a learning experience on it. We don't dwell on the past. We forge forward, just glancing in the rearview mirror. The windshield in front of us is where we are looking. The second store gave Bob an idea of how to expand. It taught him valuable lessons on how to grow and stay within your means. The bakery taught Bob the concept of giving the customers a little more than they want, sort of giving an A+ instead of an A. The negativity that Bob received from his inner voice, plus, the enthusiasm for another project created the concept of going into the catering business. This time Bob was so influenced on his past that he knew he would do well and prosper. And he did.

COMMUNITY

With the power of influence comes the awesome power and responsibility of owning a store. Which creates the power of giving back. People give money to charity all the time. Some I feel just do it to be seen. It's nice to have your name on the wall as a platinum giver, having donated $20,000 dollars to a cause. It's nice to receive awards for donating huge sums of cash and nice to have a business name slapped on a banner or neon sign at football stadium. It's another thing to donate time, for time is money. A small niche business connects with the community in small ways, yet having a positive influence on others. Summit Meats was right there, contributing time and money. Bob sponsored knothole teams, soccer teams, and he placed ads in the local Forest Hills Journal, the community paper. Bob also sponsored McNicholas High School with raising money for youth events at the school, through placing ads in the sports programs and other school functions. But this is where Bob separates himself from the others. This is why he excels at what he does. Bob gives back his time.

"Companies that encourage community involvement distinguish themselves from their competitors, and see many benefits, including loyal customers and happier employees."-

Lindsay LaVine, Entrepreneur [8]

EFFECTIVE

Bob's influence was felt throughout Summit and Anderson Twp. Sponsoring teams and events was great to get the word about Summit Meats out on the street. Bob, though, would connect with hands-on experiences and reach out to the grade schools and high schools through offering his skills to influence others on a career path, guiding others on understanding how to own a business. Summit Elementary was the school right in the middle of the nine hundred home community, Bob went there and spoke about what a butcher does. Bob had Turpin High School students come over and see what transpires at a butcher shop. He had Anderson High School kids come over and see firsthand how to prepare ground beef, cut open a chicken, create sausage links and how to make a deli sandwich. Bob was being asked to offer time and not just cash because people liked his attitude and his influence. So why not ask him to come and speak, display his passion and shed light on the business world at the local schools. We all know who Proctor and Gamble is, we know who Great American Insurance is, Gold Star Chili, Skyline Chili, Kroger and all the other great big businesses in Cincinnati are. But to see a small business in high demand creates a positive outlook for others. Creating the next Bobs, the next Bernies and of course the next Herberts of the world.

COMMUNICATION

1986 created more than supplementary commerce, it created Bob the capability to cultivate as a person, to reach out and offer his expert services to others. Catering is not easy, it's more hours, it's event planning, it's blocking out weekends, holidays and forecasting even further. But, what Bob saw, was more than riches. It was giving his customers a little extra. You don't just wake up and say "I am going into catering." Bob had so many requests that the time was just right. His background in the butcher business had served him well and customers sometimes have a far greater influence than we give them credit for. So to all the customers whom spoke, talked , lured, and of course influenced Bob into catering; I know he thanks you.

Kay Ireland from Demand Media wrote an article titled, *Why Should I Start a Catering Business?*
She listed three main reasons.

~ You love food......
~ You love people.....
~ You love freedom...[9]

EMERGING

2 for 3, that is a .666 batting average. I know that is good. As I look at those three reasons I would say Bob had two of them nailed to a T. Freedom, well owning a store and catering I don't think allowed for that much freedom. His passion for chow and for people makes up for freedom. Now for the record, Bob was not into making millions of dollars off of catering, he was not going to sell the store and just focus on catering. Bob did this to subsidize his income, provide a need and allow himself to offer additional services to his customers. There is a big difference between catering to the needs of the Kennedys vs. the needs of the Sergers. Bob's influence of the bakery and his second store allowed for him to put a visible cap on his catering business. A wedding. No problem, but it was just food. Catering to his daughter Leah's high school volleyball team—no problem. Catering to a golf outing—no problem. Catering to a sports stag—no problem. You get the idea. Summit Meats was Bob's anchor store. He was not about to lose sight of that. Catering in a simple, economical fashion is how Bob saw the catering business, yet, knowing his limitations and staying focused on the butcher shop.

Bob's freedom was limited. He had a trustworthy staff. One which would carry him while he was away on his catering business. Trust, like I noted, is key. Leaders build trust. They influence others so well that the cat and mouse game never takes place. The mice never play, for leaders create more leaders and that is what Bob did, because that is what Bernie did from the word start. Positive influence....................

"If it is to be, it is up to me!"

Author Unknown

CHAPTER 12 "JIMMY, GET YOUR BUTT IN HERE"

In 1987, I was sixteen years old. My parents bought me a 1977 Volkswagen Rabbit and yes it was a five speed manual with a moon roof. I now could drive to football practice and baseball practice. I didn't have to ride the bus, nor did I need to carpool with the older kids. I now could take the younger class to school or to practice, as some of the upper class once did for me. T.R O'Brien shuffled me home from practice all the time, so it was my turn. I would say T.R had a positive influence over me, for I now was paying it forward and I did that all the way up until I graduated in 1989.

With a car comes responsibility. With a car means you can get out and see the world first hand, drive around and make solid decisions for yourself. However, with a car comes gasoline. In order to get gas you had to have money. That Christmas my parents encouraged me to get my first job outside of my comfort zone. I landed a seasonal job with Gold Circle at Beechmont Mall. A department store. I would stock shelves, clean the floors, unload the stock and face the store. I worked there for two months, then right after the holiday rush was over my dad came up to me and stated that Earl Mette was looking for a part-time cashier. I had known Earl for years, my parents trusted him and knew he would be a tremendous boss for me at a young age.

With that piece of advice I went down to the store and spoke with Earl. We chatted for about fifteen minutes and I landed the job I would stay at until I was twenty-one. This depot I had been into over thousand times. From getting Icees after a baseball game, to getting soft service ice cream. From a beer run with my dad to just riding up on my bike with my buddies for junk food. Convenient Food Mart was an ingredient of my everyday life. My dad would stop and get coffee, gas and chewing gum before our baseball game. My mom would stop and get soda and snacks for the players after the ball game. The strip mall it seems was a part of not only my life but my buddies' parents as well. The bank, the convenience store and of course the butcher shop. It was one-stop shopping which was built on customer service. All three shops provided a need. They also provided excellent customer service which created loyal customers.

As I started my new job in a fast paced environment, it seemed I knew all the people who shopped there. Every day when people would see me, they would ask aren't you Jim Serger's son? Aren't you Marilyn Serger's son? I know you, I know your parents. Handshakes like I had never experienced in my life were transpiring. This job developed into a social experience that I never would have imagined. I was manning the cash register, creating money orders, counting cash, conducting inventory, cleaning the carpets and picking up cigarette butts off the sidewalk. I was wrapping produce. I was waiting on people, carrying out groceries, plus, holding the doors for customers. I was facing the store, I was conducting price changes and I was loving ever single minute of the experience. Earl had two sons, Brian and Kevin who I just admired so much. I worked alongside friends who I had known for years, playing baseball with them. Their dads were my coaches and now as a young adult I was working side by side with the very folks I use to build forts with, swim at the pool with or play summer ball with.

With the strip mall holding three lucrative businesses I would begin to forge a relationship with the store owners of each establishment. Of course, my first deposit was at the bank with Brad Kopf. The butcher shop. I didn't know them that well, at least as sound as the banker and

Earl. Every single day I worked an employee would walk down from the bank and I would talk with them, as I did when I entered the bank with my hard earned cash. The butcher shop was the same way. Bob would walk over and purchase a few things he needed and that was the start to something very extraordinary.

ADVICE

Bob and I would chat all the time when he was in the store, for his son Kevin and his daughter Leah went to the same high school as I did. Bob knew my dad back in school, he also knew my uncle Ken from his years at McNicholas. We would converse about teachers, football, baseball and he would always ask me how my mom and dad were. Bob knew my parents really well; sports stags at school, fund raisers, bingo night or other events they would see each other at. The nine hundred home community it seemed some days, housed just one enormous house. All living under one roof. Everybody knew each other, everybody knew each other's kids, everybody had a connection with each other bigger than Kevin Bacon could ever fathom.

As one matures, and as one soaks up influence we often hear it was an outsider who guided them the most. By far this strip mall was the biggest influence outside of my sports. I loved my sports, but I loved working, if not more. I loved speaking with people, getting to know them, listening to them and catching a glimpse of what greatness is. Bob Cappel had that influence over me. I was now eighteen years old, big time high school grad. No more summer sports, no more football. Just work and focusing on attending the University of Cincinnati. That summer I had the pleasure of being promoted to assistant manager, yes one day a week. Saturday night I would close down the store. My shift was from four p.m. until twelve midnight. With that promotion, I also was in charge of counting the register down and making the nightly deposits. The other days I was the cashier on the same shift, 4-12. No matter what, Saturdays were for working. I loved the post. I would show up an hour early and I would stay an hour late. I was being led by some fascinating people. Brad Toft, Paul Rottmueller, Johnny McManus and of course Brian, Kevin and Earl.

MEMBER

At eighteen, I now had cash and I was saving like crazy. With cash I now could afford to walk over to the butcher shop and get a meal for myself. At eighteen, a meal was really just a hearty deli sandwich and this is where my interaction with Bob would really take shape. I would chat with him all the time. We would jabber about work. We would speak about the lines I had at the counter some days. We would discuss about my day and of course he would always ask how my parents were. I would watch Bob work his magic behind the counter. I would see him move, hovering around as if in thin air. So quick on his feet, one end of the counter to the other. He knew where everything was. What stood out was every single time I walked in, he would say with a loud, stern, welcoming voice," There's Jim." The little bell would go off on the door and without any hesitation he would acknowledge me as if I was the King of England. Giving me his attention, yet still focusing on his actual duties. He would stop, walk up behind the counter and say, "What can I get you." He was placing me, the customer, the kid who he had known for years at center stage. He knew I would only spend five bucks, but to him, it appeared as if I was spending a thousand.

CONSISTENT

Attitude is a key ingredient in any industry and Bob had the attitude of placing customers first, no matter the dollar amount. Bob was creating a constructive atmosphere. For that was who Bob was. He was always buoyant and energetic. I never knew Bob was tired, I never knew Bob was under the weather. I never knew Bob needed to go home early. Bob never teeter tottered, he was always Bob to me. No mood swings like a pendulum. No Dr. Jekyll or Mr. Hyde was ever apparent to me. Bob was always true to character. He was all in. I am sure some days he had to paint a smile on, but to me it was never apparent. His staff, who I just adored, were the same way to me. Karen and Mike were always respectful of me, saying hello and meaning it. That comes from Bob giving them the same elements and influence Bernie and Herbert gave him.

Bob was giving his positive outlook onto others all the time. You could feel the liveliness in the store the moment you walked in. As Bob or Karen waited on me, the door would open and they would extend a friendly hello, with a name attached to it. If they did not know the person's name, they would say, "I am Bob, how may I help you?" His introduction and his charismatic approach was being zapped all over the store. It was radiating like a glow I had felt at the convenience store. But why? 10,000 hours plus took Bob to where he was today. He was an authority in all fields of business. Foremost, the people business. He knew he could create a demand for his food and preparation, but he had to bond with people. Bob did it so well for the past twenty-two years ever since starting at Hornschemeier Grocery. Bob new the value of placing customers foremost. 10,000 hours, was now more like 50,000 hours. He was at the height of this career path and still continuing to develop.

TRUSTWORTHY

Trust and influence are keys to business and in life. We trust others, for we comprehend they have been through numerous situations and their solid advice is taken not under consideration, but taken as golden. At the convenient store, we had a grill and we loved as a team to grill out. So one Saturday I took it upon myself to fire up the grill and cook burgers for the team. Funny part was, I had never fired up the grill. That was my dad's job and he did it well. It looked easy. So I walked over to Summit Meats and Karen waited on me. I said, I needed about ten burgers, pre-made and I was going to grill out. I told her I had never grilled out before. She stated it was easy. She told me how to do it. Take the top rack off, fill the grill with charcoal. Squirt lighter fluid on the coals, then light it. Place the rack back down and throw the burgers on. Whammo! Burgers are ready to serve. So I did as she told me, literally. I lit the coals, threw the rack on and placed the burgers on the grill. The flame went out, the charcoal was still black and the burgers sat there raw. All ten staring up at me, as to say, you idiot! So I waited a few minutes, took the burgers off and threw them away. That's it, I never grilled again for a few years.

KINSHIP

At eighteen years old you are seen as an adult. You can vote now. You are the big time. So with that, I was invited to the annual Convenient Food Mart golf outing. I got my first real chance to play alongside customers that I had known for years, the coffee clutch. The crew of about twenty men who would congregate at the store every morning for coffee, smokes and gossip. I knew them all. Some of their kids worked with me. This time I could play and have fun with them all. I respected each and every one of those men. With the eighteen holes completed, it was time to hit the 19th hole. Earl the owner drove me to the event, and low and behold we went to a park. Open air, horseshoes, picnic tables, and a few grills. As we pulled up there was a man who was manning his battle station. Bob Cappel, Saturday, mid-afternoon, behind the grill firing up steaks and burgers. The butcher, the caterer, the gentleman whose store was in high demand on Saturdays was there performing his practice. For the men playing golf were also his customers. Earl knew the price of excellent service, the importance of excellent food. So who do you call for such an occasion? Bob. This went on every year the outing took place. Earl was so influenced by Bob's demeanor that Bob had to be there, and he was. The food was outstanding and of course Bob and I would talk and talk.

Saturdays were a sound day for a butcher shop, but Bob knew it was only one Saturday a year and he was going to be there. Giving customers more is what Bob did all the time. Plus, one day was not a big deal. So yes, Bob gave back to the people who gave him so much. We all know what a compass is; North, South, East and West. For Walt Disney it was; Needs, Stereotypes, Emotions and Wants. Bob knew the four keys to customer service very well, it's called a "Compass Rose." Bob new the track of his store, he knew where he was taking the store and with that his team as well.

In an article by Fast Company; Nick Nanton and JW Dicks write on Disney Customer-Care Philosophy.

What stood out were seven sides to service as it pertains to the seven dwarfs.

—Be Happy...make eye contact and smile.

—Be like Sneezy....greet and welcome each and every client. Spread the spirit of hospitality...it's   contagious!

—Don't be Bashful....seek out client contact.

—Be like Doc.......provide immediate service recovery.

—Don't be Grumpy......always display appropriate body language at all times.

—Be like Sleepy......create dreams and preserve the magical client experience.

—Don't be Dopey.....thank each and every customer![10]

BUILDING

Bob Cappel was the influence created by positive influence, however Bob still had to take control of his business. Influence can only take us so far in life, the rest is up to us. People say I thank God for all of my blessings. Well, I think we also need to thank ourselves. The Bible is a great guide, but in order for it to work we have to make a decision on our own to follow it. God's grace only takes shape if we make a choice to follow the scriptures. God gives 100% effort and guidance, but we make the decisions here on earth to do what is right and what is wrong. We never give ourselves enough credit. In order for something to be 100%, we have to give 100%. If we slip up, sell off a business, try our best at a niche shop and close the doors after a triumphant effort, we still forge on. We don't give up the ship on the first sign of water intake. We make mistakes. We try our own creations. We have our own inventions, we have our own feelings, our own work ethic and all of those derived from others who we have interacted with. They are the very people who shape us and mold us into what we are, yet "WE" still have to create our own outlook and our own visions. Success isn't because someone else created you, it's because you took others' knowledge; mended it, altered it, and made your own statue with advice and input from others. Ultimately it's us who create our own success.

CHARISMA

I treasured working Saturday nights at the store. Some nights we were just slammed and other nights it seemed we were the only ones around. So as a team, we would do some pretty crazy things; aisle football, crank the music up while cleaning or see how many Icees we could gulp down in a row. We always seemed though to venture out back. Earl and Brian loved to participate in wiffleball games on stock day. On many a nights, the crew and I would head out back and get in a few swings. One night I chose the wrong night, and sure enough we all were out back except the one cashier we left alone. We left the back door ajar so we could hear the buzzer to call us up front for assistance. Well, the game was just too intense. We forgot about our job and focused in on the competition. With that, the back door of Summit Meats swung open and I heard. "Jimmy, get your butt up front." I looked back and sure enough it was Bob. He was not screaming at me, but he was taken back as to what was transpiring. We all dropped what we were doing and headed right in. A long, single file line, at least forty people deep had been constructed. It took us a little over an hour to get the line down. Both cash registers in full throttle, customers angry at me. They had every right. I put my needs first instead of theirs. A little while longer after the rush was gone, Bob ventured over. He walked in with a smile from ear to ear. He never spoke of the incident, but he just said, "Jimmy, how you doing over here?" He never scolded me, yelled at me or embarrassed me. He just gave me the look of, "you are better than that". He never mentioned it again and it never ever happened again.

EFFECTIVE

Fun is what being at work should be. Love what you do so much that you get paid for doing what you love. Bob knew I loved work, he also spoke to me as a man and not as a child. I had the highest respect for Bob. On my daily drive back from college classes I would stop in and grab a sandwich. Pastrami with onions, lettuce, mustard, wheat bread and a pickle. All for a few bucks. I did that all the time. I would stop in. Looking back, I think I just stopped in to just say hi. I felt comfort at that store, I felt protected at that store. Bob was always working in the white apron with stains all over him, yet he was always in a great mood. He would be working with blood and guts in the back, yet still ask how I am doing. Bob was a man who I looked forward to speaking with, who through his actions were shaping me into a man at the young age of twenty-one in 1992.

Influence
Drop a pebble in the water,
And its ripples reach out far;
And the sunbeams dancing on them
May reflect then to a star.
Give a smile to someone passing,
Thereby making his morning glad;
It may greet you in the evening
When your own heart may be sad.
Do a deed of simple kindness;
Though its end you may not see,
it may reach, like widening ripples,
Down a long eternity.[11]

Joseph Morris

CHAPTER 13 PENNY KNOWS BEST

SHARE

Every day I worked at the convenience store I would exchange conversation for at least 15 minutes with Bob, whether he was in the store or I was in the butcher shop. In December, 1991 I earned my associates degree and I signed up for the Navy. I would leave in April of 1992. In January and February I would work fulltime at the store. I would now open the store up at 0600; maybe to prepare myself for getting up early. Either way, I would now see Bob before the butcher shop would even open. There he was, game face on. Then again, his game face was always the same to me, good mood and driven to take on the day's challenges. Already to tackle the day. What I found interesting was Bob was the same in the morning as he was in the evening. His attitude, his outlook, his character elements were just as radiant to me at 0600 as they were at 1800 when the store was closing down. Bob was a man I looked forward to seeing ever day. Bob presented himself with a zip in his step and always seemed to have a smile. No matter the time, the day, the week. Rain, snow, sleet, hail. Christmas, Thanksgiving, Easter, graduation weekend; it didn't matter. Bob never displayed what I would call a weakness. That is why I look back and see how to present myself. Bob's habits were off the charts, Bob's motivation was off the charts and Bob's speaking abilities were off the charts. I know I was only 21 years old; but inspiration is soaked in at a young age.

Approachable

April 26, 1992 I left for my four year stint in the Navy. I moved to Japan and would not come home for two years. In summer of 1994, I came back to Cincinnati, back to Summit Estates and back to my parents house for thirty days of leave. I did not have a car, but what I could do was walk. After a few days off being home, settling down and getting into a routine, I started walking down to the butcher shop for lunch. A half mile walk or so for a Colby cheese, salami sandwich with all the fixings. I did that for just about three weeks. What is fascinating about a positive relationship is that it never seems to end. You just pick right up where you left off, and without any hesitation, that is what Bob and I did. He asked all about my career. I asked how his son Kevin was doing and his daughter Leah as well as Bobby, his youngest. We spoke on where I have been and where I lived. All the while he was working his magic behind the counter. Still wearing his stained apron and still light on his feet, Bob would still find a few minutes to create me a mouth watering sandwich. Converse with great zest, show his compassion towards me and in 15 minutes or so I would start my walk back to the house. Habits never die and never fade away. We create prudent habits and those shine through and all take notice. Summit Meats was still booming, still going strong, and Bob; as if he was the energizer bunny, was stilling going and going.

In 1996 I left the Navy, and of course, I moved back home. I took 20 days off and started what would be a eighteen year career with Home City Ice. After landing the job, I would live with my parents for 5 months, create a foundation and eventually move out. With delivering ice, I was able to get a route in Anderson Twp, and with that route I was able to stop in the shop and eat lunch. I could have gone to McDonald's, Hardee's or Gold Star. But I wanted to give my money to Bob. I wanted him to have it. For I knew when I walked in he would treat me like a person and not a number. I would park my huge truck out front and hustle in. Bob would stop what he was doing and create a superb sandwich. He would ask where I was going, how late I was working, how are my mom and dad and so on. He seemed always intuitive as to what I was doing. Maybe he did this with all of his customers. To me, Bob gave me center stage every time I proceeded through he doors.

1996 was a big year for me. Getting out of the Navy, moving home and creating a new outlook on my life was to take shape. When I was interviewed for the job with Home City Ice, I met my wife Tarla. She was the secretary and on coming home I told my brother I would marry that girl. He looked at me as if I was crazy, turns out she lived in Anderson and went to Anderson high school. She was one year younger.

It would take me two years just to ask her out on a date. Sure enough, a Christmas party was just the plan. So we started dating and in 1999 I would ask her to marry me. Our wedding was set for March 25, 2000.

LISTEN

We never know who will influence us, we never know how or why. But we just listen to them. Penny, Bob's wife was just that influence he needed. You see, in 1996 Bob had the concept of selling his store. Having been an excellent ride, Bob just thought it was time to sell off what it created, Summit Meats. Twenty years in the business, twenty years of commitment, twenty years of triumph it just seemed right to Bob to clear his table and start another journey. Yet, Penny had a different vision. She explained to Bob that the timing was just not right. She explained to him that Bob could offer his qualities for a few more years, then when he felt it was time, sell. Penny's influence on Bob helped guide him to six more years of community service, six more years of creating magic on the community. Bob and Penny have a relationship as husband and wife that is very inviting, with an open honest relationship. Bob and Penny were now in their late 40's. Bob was starting to feel a little fatigued, little run down. Bob's body was staring to ache. Not bad, but he could feel it in his knees and lower back. Yet a few aspirin and he was off to the races. Bob took Penny up on her recommendation and continued to keep the butcher shop open. The 900 home community was not quite as booming as it had been, the convenience store that was the anchor had sold off to a new tenant. Foot traffic was coming to minimum. Occupants over twenty years were moving out of Summit and heading to smaller homes. Their kids who road bikes were now having kids themselves and were moving further out east. Summit was beginning to slow down rapidly. The original homeowners were now in their 50's and the empty nesters seemed to be everywhere.

Loyal

In 1994, the convenient food mart sold off, but what kept going annually was the golf outing and I was not going to miss out. Tom Myrick, Al Bowe, Earl Mette, Joe Ryan, Chuck Heckler and a ton of others just would not allow that special occasion to sliver away. Memories last a life time, so they continued to keep the outing going. With the outing of course came food and who do think was right there at the 19th hole???? Bob and his special skills. Just like Liam Neeson in the movie Taken, Bob as well had a certain set of skills. Those skills were slowing down as I noted, but loyal customers still continued to give Bob their business. A niche business is not easy, for today Americans want it all under one roof. As a loyal customer, I was not about to give a stranger my business, the business of catering my wedding.

In 1999 I asked Tarla to marry me and with that the wedding plans took shape. The first person I thought of was Bob Cappel. Tarla and I started setting everything up; church, reception hall, honeymoon, wedding party and of course the caterer. We would invite 150 people which quickly turned into 200. I knew I had to get a hold of Bob and right away I raced down to Summit Meats and spoke with him. Sure enough, without any hesitation he said yes. Our wedding was on the west side of town, over 20 miles away from Summit Meats. Bob didn't care. He was going to do it. I'm never one to worry about very much, I trust people maybe a little too much. I knew my family and friends were in good hands, I knew they would enjoy the food and would savor the moment. That day went by so fast, I hardly remember the evening. But what I do remember is Bob was there. The very man who I cared for and looked up to was offering his services to my guests. What I had experienced with Mr. Cappel over the past years, people were enjoying, people were devouring, and the compliments poured in over the next few days, months and even years. Bob's skills that evening weren't surprising to me, I had known he was great, but for others to comment on his meal is how you know you are really special.

APPRECIATIVE

None of that would have taken place had not one person influenced another. Penny's positive reinforcements created Bob being at my wedding, it created a special moment in my life. The man whom I spoke with every single day, the man who joked with me, watched me grow and develop into a man was able to offer his skills to me. I thanked Bob over and over that night. Even his daughter Leah was there, a family business meant more to that day than any other day. Summit Meats, Bob and his staff were there because a long time ago Bernie influenced Bob. We never know what tomorrow is going to bring, yet through positive habits we create our own destiny. Bob affected his destiny because he knew others shape our lives into what we are. We listen to our inner voice, yet console others on advice. We listen well. We follow a good clean moral path and watch our successes take off like a rocket ship.

ETHICS

Bob formed a great habit years ago, long before my wedding day. He formed it through others guiding him and nurturing him, through watching his dad fix a leaky faucet, through watching Bernie place ad signs in the windows for the weekly specials. Bob's habits were created through the eyes of himself watching others actions. Good habits created a success in a niche business, but more importantly, Bob created more Bob's. Yes, there are no waves of Bob's on a distant planet ready to zoom down and roam the earth. Bob, through his guidance, wisdom, charisma, and ethical upbringing created influence on me and others. His son Kevin is a success with a major beer supplier. His daughter Leah is a success as a mom and through her work ethic with the packaged goods industry. His youngest, Bobby, is a success as a manager with a printing company. The three learned from Bob because Bob learned from others. The three were working at Summit Meats as kids, as teenagers and through college. They grew positive traits that have guided them on their path. Penny as well guided Bob through constructive habits, through cheering her companion on, through watching his P&L statements and I am sure telling him to tone it down a bit on

100 Next In Line Please

spending or any other element that needed watching over.

The Habit
I am your constant companion,
I am your greatest helper or heaviest burden.
I will push you onward or drag you down to failure.
I am completely at your command.
Half the things you do might just as well turn over to me
and I will be able to do them quickly and correctly.
I am easily managed-
you must merely be firm with me.
Show me exactly how you want something done
and after a few lessons, I will do it automatically.
I am the servant of all great people;
and alas, of all failures as well.
Those who are great,
I have made great.
Those who are failures,
I have made failures.
I am not a machine,
though I work with all the precision of a machine
plus the intelligence of a human.
You may run for a profit or run me for ruin-
it makes no difference to me.
Take me,
train me,
be firm with me,
And I will place the world at your feet.
Be easy with me,
and I will destroy you.
Who am I?
I AM A HABIT.

Unknown

CHAPTER 14 START WITH THE END IN MIND

EFFECTIVE

Herbert Cappel molded a young man through positive guidance and through positive influence. I am not going to say that Bob had an easy life, that it was a cake walk. Nothing worth receiving is, unless it is handed to you on a silver platter. Herbert displayed what success is to a young boy, a teenager and to a young man. Bob picked up those traits and ran as fast as he could. Herbert created a gentleman, business owner and loving husband and dad because he knew that was his responsibility as a father. We all know success is difficult to explain, for we all see success differently. One has dollar figures, one has a big title; yet I don't think that defines success. Herbert saw Bob as a success long before Bob did, or anyone else for that matter. Herbert created a boy into a man who was not afraid of fear and one that was not afraid of giving more effort. A man that would not take handouts and one that would create his own niche on this planet. Herbert molded Bob, not Bob the butcher. But Bob, the man who shows us the way, for he is the way. CEO, President, VP; all of them are grand titles. Herbert, through his guidance, taught Bob that success is more than a title, it's about creating an impact on others through actions. It's about creating more leaders and entrepreneurs by showing them through displaying what it means to care for others. To place others first. To work hard. To achieve greatness because we want to, not because we feel we have to. The big difference between a butcher and an insurance salesman; blood and guts vs. suit and tie. In reality, on the back end, they are the same; speaking, interacting, planning, forecasting and most of all forming good solid working habits. These things are what makes us a success.

In 2002 Bob decided the time was the right to close the doors on a success story. Steven Covey had a best seller called 7 Habits of Highly Effective People. One of the traits was, start with the end in mind, i.e, know how you want to close the book before the book is even started. Bob's book was opened and closed by creating a business through passion and hard work. It opened with a smile on his face and it closed creating a smile for over twenty-five years. Nothing in life is painless. Sacrifice and long hours seven days a week. But in order to create something out of nothing, we have to put aside luxuries in order to obtain luxuries. Let's see, Bob opened the store when he was twenty-seven and closed the store down when he was fifty-three. Having owned the store for over twenty-five years I am sure he created a few dents in life. Can't make it to all the kid's games. Can't make it to all the kids plays. Can't make it to all the parties. But with sacrifice at an early stage in one's career, it opens a door for greener pastures in the future. At fifty-three Bob sold the store for a significant amount, far greater than what he imagined when he was just twenty-seven. What Bob did was see a future that often we don't see, we are so wrapped up in wanting more that we lose sight of why we opened a business or started a journey in the first place.

PURSUIT

Who thought that creating a deli tray could be lucrative? Who thought that cracked pepper mill turkey breast could be a beloved passion? Provolone cheese could pay bills, Swiss and Gouda cheese could pay for a catholic education for his kids. Who would have thought that terminology such as beta-carotene, vitamin E, omega-3, hormones, free range, shin, leg flank could create a business for twenty-five years. I will tell you who, Herbert Cappel. Bob's dad saw this end a long, long time ago. Well before Bob ever met Penny. Long before Bob met Dan and long before Herbert met his wife Marie. Herbert knew that hard work would only take him so far in life, but hard work and passion are unbeatable. I recognize a butcher is not a dream trade nowadays for college grads or high school kids. Technology is the current wave, so who is going to filet steaks? Who is going to slaughter cows, who is going to raise cattle? I'll tell you who, the young man or young woman who follow their dream. The ones who are led to water and take a drink because they are encouraged to do what they love. Bob created his own niche in life, because he had parents who cheered him on. He had parents who guided him, yet allowed him to construct decisions for himself. One store was sold and the other closed, so what. At least he tried. Do you remember the chap who gave up after failing twice, or further? I don't. I know greats as Steve Jobs, Michael Jordan, Albert Einstein, Abraham Lincoln and Martin Luther King. They all faced setbacks. They by no means stopped their pursuit. They completed what they started and today those beliefs are still guiding others and reassuring others to continue to keep going. Bob Cappel is not a household name, but to me he is. To me he is larger than Mickey Mantle. More superior than Chris Sabo. Bigger than Pete Rose. He impacted my life daily throughout my teenage days and young adult years.

Help

Today at forty-four, I tell a surplus of stories that happened to me before the age of twenty-five. I vividly remember the day Bob came over and asked for aid in the evening prior to Thanksgiving. His truck was delayed due to horrific weather and sure enough, he asked for assistance. I was cashiering and Kevin my supervisor said that was okay. Sure enough, late into the evening I was there unloading turkeys. I learned about teamwork and about what it meant to help your neighbor. What it meant to lend a hand even though it was not my job. I remember the day Bob got his MAC machine or a ATM. It was a big deal. I could use my credit card for purchases. In reality what Bob was teaching me was giving your customers a little more.

In the Business News Daily, there was an article written by David Mielach called The No. 1 Reason People Sell a Business. Here lists a few reasons.

Avoid tax charges

Retire

Burnout[12]

He goes on to state, "Baby boomers represent more than half of the business owners in the U.S. and many are selling their business in order to have a comfortable retirement." Half are baby boomers. So what does our future look like once the Bob's retire? Having a business, owning a business is a magnificent accomplishment. It takes more than capital to flourish. It takes more than collaboration to thrash the elements and it takes more than leadership to keep it going for over twenty-five years. In 2002, it just seemed right for Bob and Penny to sell the store off. The neighborhood was slowing down and some days when I drove through I wouldn't even see a youngster on a bike. Times were a changing, as Bob Dylan would sing it. People were moving on, Bob comprehend that. He took the lead and sold off. Today Summit Meats is still open. It's still located in the same location where Dan and Bob built their treasure. The Convenience store is long gone, now a flower shop. The bank had since moved years ago. Relocating to Nagel Road. A busier street.

EFFECTIVELY

Bob's dream of owning a store had come to halt. In reality, it never stops success. When folks talk about your business for years and years. It was a success. Bob though, could have gone into the used car business and would have done fine. He could have been in the pharmaceutical field and would have done remarkable. Bob was an expert in his field because Bob didn't stand still. He kept moving, kept gaining knowledge and continued to create a need and a want for his products. Bob would have made anything turn to gold because he wanted to succeed and succeed he did. A butcher is an occupation that is not being pursued nor spoke of today. I don't hear college kids say, "I can't wait to be a butcher."

The end in mind is a lesson for us all. Bob and Dan created a thriving business in the meat world. Fashioned a thriving business in the cheese world and banked on cook outs, parties, holidays and graduations to make ends meet. They both flourished because they worked well together and were buddies through habits created years ago.

CREATE

Bob's store closed its doors in 2002. Yet, here in Carmel, Indiana where I live a butcher shop opened its doors in 2006. Joe's Butcher Shop. Joe Lazzara, a man similar to Bob. Joe's grandparents ran a Sicilian fruit and vegetable market. Good quality food, customer service and community involvement were apparent. Joe's mom and dad taught him a value at a young age to give back to the community. So having been around that environment for years, plus Joe's background in the business sector, cultivated the concept of a butcher shop. Joe noticed that the big stores weren't offering more than just meat. The product knowledge was missing, the passion was missing and the connecting with locals were missing. The very thing that Summit Meats had, Joe is creating in Carmel. Joe's efforts created a niche business in Carmel. He created a need and a want. People needed quality products, so they wanted to go to Joe's Butcher Shop for their products. It's 2015 and the habits Joe was taught through his mom and dad are still flourishing here in Carmel. The fresh beef, veal, lamb, pork, sausages, chicken are the same quality as Bob's store. The two men had the same vision and the same passion. Put people first and the rest will take care of itself. Don't be stagnant. Create more, offer more and be better than yesterday. Joe and Bob would have been buddies. Joe's shop is going on ten years old. Awesome. Joe is now in the delivery service and in the fish business as well. Joe continues to be creative as did Bob. Both men set the bar high on what is means to overcome fear and open a shop. They started with the end in mind, give and give and give......one story had ended, but one story is growing.

"Remember that guy that gave up? Neither does anyone else."

Unknown

CHAPTER 15 TODAY

GAINING

In 2002 Bob sold off his prized possession. He loved the store a great deal but it was time for Bob to take a back seat again. Or so he thought. I guess once an owner always an owner. Once an entrepreneur, always an entrepreneur. Bob was no different. Only taking a few months off and gathering his thoughts, Bob again was out and about roaming the culinary world. Bob took his skills to Sam's Club. He wanted to feel the ins and outs of a major store, he lasted all of four months. Small vs. big just was not Bob's niche. He loved the connection part of Summit Meats. Bob was even given the chance to go into business with another shop. This time he pulled out in the nick of time due to speculation. The expert listened to his gut instinct and sure enough a few months later the shop was up for sale.

Once an entrepreneur, always an entrepreneur. Bob loved the freshness of opening a new store, the freshness of a challenging concept and the passion for ownership. So, like old times, Bob tried his hand again with another shop. This time close to his old stomping grounds as a young lad, Pleasant Ridge. He would pursue leasing a section of a community market, which was an old IGA store. Bob would create a butcher themed section of the store and bring his elements back to center stage which would forge a demand for his skills once again. However, after seven months, the rent, electric and a slew of other needs were jacked way up. Bob knew he was not going to buy the property so he once again folded his cards and stepped away from that project. He stepped away because he put his family first. For years it was always customers first but this time he put his family first. A dream had already been created, owning his own store. He had already gone through achieving his goal and he was content, understanding that creating another dream was not that vital for him.

Bob loves the schematics of the meat industry. With the store, he understood what the demands of owning a business could do to a family. He was fifty-six years old and wise enough to take a step back and revaluate his intentions in life and in business. For a small number of years, Bob dabbled with opening another shop, working in a big store and was even offered a grand job with a premium meat and cheese company. Bob's needs were in demand. Bob's work habits, though, were even more in demand. Everyone knew Bob's story. When you are in the business, people know who you are through word of mouth. People know you are first-rate and businesses want your talent. How cool is that. People want you.

Family
Bob worked at Paula's, formally Bracke Meats for four months, then off to Humber Meats for two and half years. Then off to Fresh Market for six years. Bob's father created that pattern. Bob's early mentor Bernie, created that configuration. Retiring is not in Bob's vocabulary, not even after he sold his business. He just loved the industry, but being the boss was long ago. He understood that. Not that he couldn't do it again, it was because he understood family comes first. I spoke to Bob quite a few times about what is imperative in his life and quickly he said his family. For years Bob had his dream in the front row, now his dreams are in the rear upper balcony. Bob's priorities are his wife, kids and without a doubt his grandkids. Some days, while I was on the

phone with Bob he had to go early, so he would go watch his daughter Leah's kids. Our conversation cut short. He knew his mission for the day. The grandkids. He so looked forward to those days of the week he noted. One day we spoke on the phone and I could hear the kids laughing and playing in the background. Bob knows where he stands today. He knows what got him to this stage of his life. His astuteness created where he lays his head at night. Others though are important to him, especially his family. I know he learned that at a young age and those values carry him to where he is today. A proud husband, father and grandpa.

We really never call it quits in life, we just create another chapter. Bob's chapters continue to produce and at the age of sixty-six I feel Bob has reached another pinnacle in his life. An all time high. He has no regrets, nothing to be grumpy about and nothing to be ashamed of. He is just as happy, if not more today than the day he and Dan opened Summit Meats.

CHAPTER 16 THE SIX MILLION DOLLAR MAN

J im, I have to have knee surgery." Yes, all those years of standing and moving ever so quickly and vigorously finally caught up to Bob. Sixty-six years old and having to lay in a hospital bed or lay on the couch at home with his knee elevated. Having to place ice packs to bring down the swelling was not Bob. This is Bob we are talking about. Having a part time job currently at the new Fresh Thyme Market with a knee brace on and driving over to watch his grandkids after school is Bob. Customer service at its finest. Placing others first.

STRONG

Bob told me a story, that I have told now over a dozen times. He was setting up a major catering gig one morning for an evening delivery. He was so wrapped up and focusing on the customer. He would close the shop down, then take the food over for delivery. Like he had done over a thousand times. Safety is at the forefront of any business and a butcher shop even more so. On this occasion Bob let a knife get away from him, causing him to cut a huge gash into his abdomen.

Luckily, he was just about wrapped up with the order. He rushed over to Anderson Mercy Hospital and proceeded to have a handful of stitches placed. Then, he headed back to the shop after a few hours, picked up the chow and still made the time deadline for the meal. That is Bob today, as it was back in the limelight. Always thinking of others, following through with a promise and following up with an excellent meal for his customers. On time, every time.

Like Steve Austin, Bob Cappel had to be rebuilt. The knee surgery, the stitches are small little glitches in his life. Like Col. Steve Austin, Bob reached for the stars. He was willing to go further. He was willing to take a risk at a young age. He was willing to face fear and overcome it. He was willing to dabble in different niche businesses, he was willing to try new adventures, yet not sacrificing who he was; a man of sheer willpower. Determination is not a gift, it's a trait we are taught at a young age. Like Steve Austin, Bob Cappel was built for success. His dad guided him and created a machine. A machine based on ethics. Based on giving it all you have. It all happened at an early age. The age of when a young son watched his dad and hero display the same traits Bob displayed to me.

Variety

We all impact each other's lives. There is a math equation that states we can interface with as much as 88,000 people in our life time. That's 3 new people per day x 365 days x 80 years. I know I have had a impact on others lives, and of course you know Bob has. But we never truly know who will pick up on our traits, who will thank us in our future. Or who will write a book about us one day. I work at the Indianapolis Airport. I interact with over five hundred plus people a day. I worked for Home City Ice for eighteen years and the amount of people I interfaced with, were in the thousands. Working in the navy, college, fraternity house, high school, sports, my family, through my writing, through my daughters school and of course through my wife being a teacher. I know I have brushed the 40,000 mark. Bob has passed the 100,000 mark. That is why we have to be role models at all times, we have to be at the ready. Everyone is watching our every move. They see us, hear us and sometimes mimic us.

If you are late to work, then don't complain when your staff is. If you don't work holidays, then don't whine when others don't want to either. You set the illustration for others to achieve greatness. Bob is no different than you and I. Bob is a man, but Bob achieved greatness because Bob wanted to. He was not given a million bucks. Bob worked his butt off to get where he is today. But what I have learned from Bob are these traits. Apply them, work on them, and watch your life change.

Don't be fearful.
Follow your dreams.
Don't be afraid to fail.
Speak with people, not at them.
Think outside the box.
Don't limit yourself.
Put customers first.
Don't get comfortable.
Think BIGGER.
Don't sit on the sidelines, be in the game of life.
Start early and go for it.
Don't worry about what others say.
Listen to your heart.
Love your kids.
Love your wife.
You can own your own business.
Never stop moving, be active.
Love your employees.
Find your one thing and do it well.
Be a cheerleader.
Don't mow down others' dreams.
Be happy with what you do.
Don't worry about titles.
Small business is lucrative.
Be around your grandkids.
Create positive memories.
Never lose sight on what's important.
Be the positive influence.
The one that really needs to be expressed is,

LOVE WHAT YOU DO SO MUCH. YOU MAKE A LIVING OUT OF IT.

CHAPTER 17 RIPPLES GO ON FOREVER. NEVER ENDING

I hope this book enabled you to understand that in order to be successful, you and you only must take the bull by the horns and go out and get it done. I had to write "Ripples" because there really is no end, we just start another chapter and so this book will end on this note. The ripples go on forever, never allow them to stop. If we don't encourage, it will stop. Take note and cheer others on. Root for the little guy. Root for the ones who others don't believe in. We never know ones capability until we allow them to grow. Add water to their life. Nurture them, comfort them, encourage them. Challenge them to improve. Be a little pushy. Don't accept average. We all make a difference in this world. We have far more effect on others than we think. Show the way.

Be the way. Laugh, have fun and don't be too serious. Take risks. Move out of state or move out of the country. Find your niche. Bob, the butcher did. You can as well. Just get started. Someone once encouraged you, so encourage someone else. If no one encouraged you, then start the ripple effect and encourage others. But really, we all have been encouraged. Help others achieve their goals, their dreams and watch them prosper. Don't stop what is in motion. For there is always someone waiting in line that would be grateful for your astuteness and support. Grasp the concept of **"Next in line please!"** Don't hesitate. Gravitate to others. As Bob did with me.

Greg Gutfeld had this advice for the 2015 college grads, I will pass along to you. **"Take any job, any job you can find. Work your butt off for one solid decade. That will put you ten years up on any pothead, backpacking-to-Europe, video-game-playing drone who thinks success drops out of the sky like a magical Kardashian....Hard work beats those who prefer identity over industry."**

CHAPTER 18 THANK YOU, MR. C

PART ONE

To Herbert Cappel,
    I never had the privilege to meet you in person, nor did I have the honor to shake your hand. But, I did have the honor of writing this book on your son. I can tell you this, having never met you, is that your son is a success because of you. It all starts at the beginning. The early stages in life; where we show compassion, we show love and most of all where we develop children into who they become. You were a strong father, a strong husband and by all means were the brick and mortar to Bob's early life. You set the tone through your habits of hard work and by your traits of what being a excellent husband, father, grandpa and friend should be. Your son is a success, and I am happy to tell you that, with the utmost respect. Your son is a success because of what he gave others: the power of positive influence. I thank you for teaching your son what it means to succeed in life. For I and thousands of others, know Bob is a success, a huge success.

PART TWO

To Bob Cappel,

It's hard to comprehend why people think others are successful in life. We compare our lives to others. Seeing if what we are doing is correct or incorrect. There is no perfect path to success, no open and closed book on what success should look like. Knowing that, success is seen differently and knowing that success is difficult to describe. I want you to know that you are a success. Through you opening up the book on your life to me, I have been able to see even more, why I admire you. I have admired you since I was a teenager. By writing this book and looking deeper, I know why I admire you. This book enhanced why I wrote it in the first place. I wanted others to see what I saw, a man who is a gentleman and a leader on and off the court. I know your dad is looking down from heaven and is smiling from ear to ear. He is very proud of you, he loves you a ton and is proud to call you his son. Long before I asked you about this project. Long before you opened Summit Meats, your dad knew you were a success. He saw it in your eyes, saw it in your habits, saw it in your personal drive and saw it in your skill set. Your success came from your efforts. Your dad guided you, but your accomplishments ultimately came from you. Because of positive influence, you were guided and achieved greatness. You are an amazing man Mr. C.

The day I came over to your house was even more impressive. We talked and talked as if we never stopped seeing each other. I live in Carmel, Indiana and you in Cincinnati. But that day, it just seemed to click again, as in days past. We picked up where we left off. I was so happy to see you and I felt so comfortable there in your home. What was so memorable about that day was not you and I talking, but what you did for others; your grandkids. We walked out back, and there in the middle of the yard, from tree to tree, was a zipline you had built. It must have been over 150 feet long. Once again, proving what I have established in this book, you always put others first. That's why you are a success. You aren't selfish, you are not egotistical or self-centered. You always consider yourself second and others first. That's why you are a winner in the game of life.

REFERENCES

1. Tom Connellan, The 1% Solution. Peak Performance Press, pg. 83
2. Outliers, Malcom Gladwell. Back Bay Books.
3. www.parents.com/parenting/better-parenting/advise/5-values-you-should-teach-your-child-by-age-five/
4. www.enquirer.com/1999/07/01/loc_cincinnatis_century.html
5. www.inc.com/guides/201101/top-10-reasons-to-own-your-own-business.html
6. www.entrepreneur.com/article/249592
7. www.forbes.com/sites/ericwagner/2013/09/12/five-reasons-8-out-of-10-businesses-fail/
8. www.entrepeneur.com/article/226974
9. smallbusiness.chron.com/should-start-catering-business-16897.html
10. www.fastcompany.com/3005566/taking-direction-disneys-customer-care-pilosophy.
11. www.inspirationalstories.com/poem/influence-joseph-norris-poem/
12. www.businessnewdaily.com/3555-business-owner-sale.html

* All **BOLD** words are by-products of Influence.

RECOMMENDED READING

Extreme Dreams Depend on Teams ~Pat Williams
The Dip ~Seth Godin
The 1% Solution ~Tom Connellan
Outliers: The Story of Success ~Malcolm Gladwell
How To Be Like Walt ~Pat Williams
Not Cool ~Greg Gutfeld
Step Up and Play Big ~Chris Ruisi
The 7 Habits of Highly Effective People ~Stephen R. Covey
QBQ! Question Behind the Question ~John G. Miller
It's Not Who You Know, It's Who You Are ~Pat Williams
Quit Your Day Job! ~Jim Denney

ACKNOWLEDGEMENTS

First off, I would like to thank Mr. Cappel. It's not every day that someone reaches out to you and asks to write a book about you. However, you were up for the challenge and I thank you for saying yes. It was fun to speak with you, recollect about our past, laugh and have fun while developing this into a book. This book was more than just a project, it was another positive impact you had on my life. I had never written a book about someone before, so I want to say thanks for allowing me to create this. Once again, because of you, I learned more about myself in writing this. I overcame the fear of reaching out to someone and writing a book about them.

To Penny Cappel. I thank you as well for your input on this book. You were the push I needed to develop it from the early stages, to what you have in your hands. Thank you for all the pointers and photo selections.

To Leah, Kevin and Bobby. Thank you for sharing your insight on your dad. For sharing photos and stories that I used. I know you love your dad very much, and he loves you all even more.

To Red Bike Publishing. Once again, thank you for creating these pages into a extraordinary end product. Thank you for believing in me and for taking on this mission. Your knowledge of the publishing industry is radiant.

To my editor, KS. Thank you for all of your input and your honesty. You are a true wordsmith. I so look forward to working on another project with you.

To my parents, Jim and Marilyn. Thank you for your positive influence and for pushing me to do more. I love you both so much.

To my wife and daughter, Tarla and Maggie. Thank you for giving me so much more than I deserve. You both inspire me to work harder and to achieve more. I love you both and enjoy my life with you so very much.

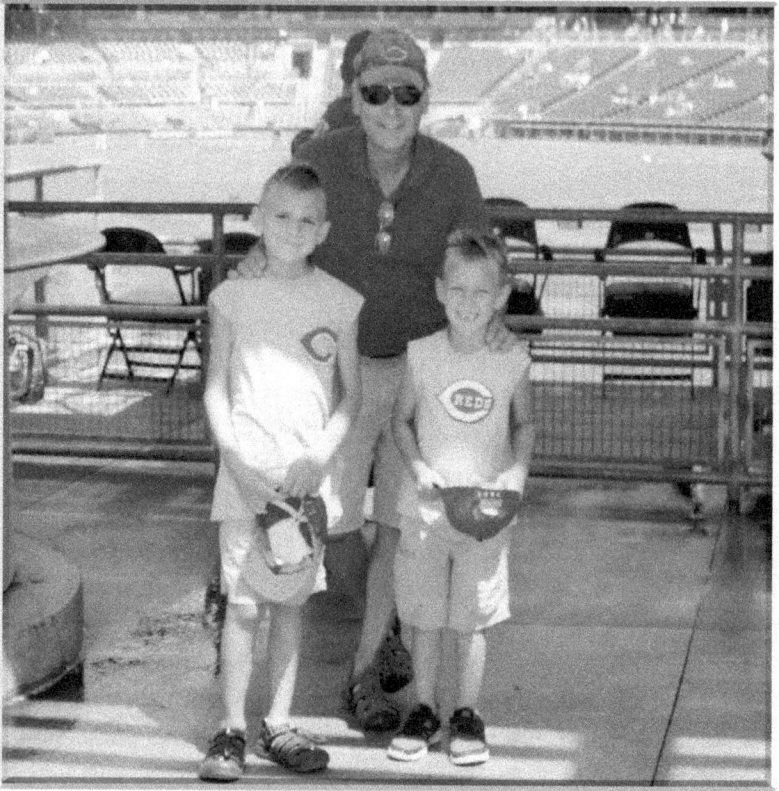

Bob and the grandkids at Great American Ball Park. Keeping the tradition alive and well. Go Reds!

Bob surrounded by his 5 grandkids. His wife Penny and daughter Leah.

Nothing will slow Bob down. Throw a knee brace on and spend time with the grandkids.

Bob and Penny with the grandkids at Disney. October, 2015.

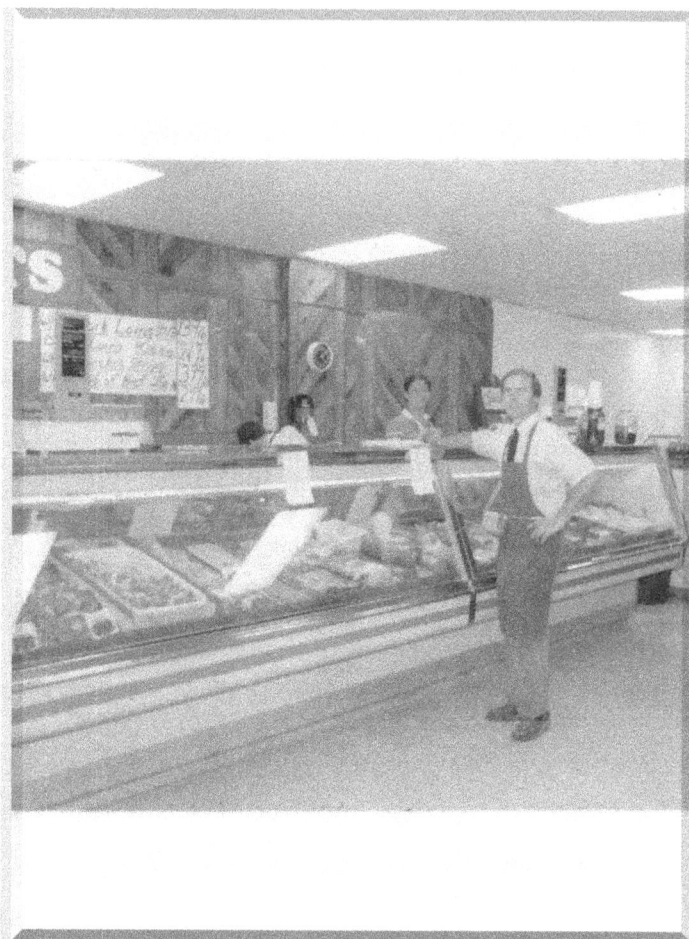

Bob in his apron. He wouldn't have it any other way. This is how Summit Estates saw Mr. Cappel. Out in front, putting customers first.

ABOUT THE AUTHOR

Jim Serger currently is in his second year with G2 Secure staff, as a operations manager at the Indianapolis Airport. Overseeing two hundred plus people in various stations. From skycaps to baggage service office, wheelchairs, aircraft cleaners, dispatchers, airline coordinators, charter flights and numerous other positions. Jim worked in the packaged ice industry for 18 years, as a plant manager and zone manager. Jim graduated from the University of Cincinnati and is a Delta Tau Delta Fraternity member. After college, Jim did four years in the U.S. Navy. Living in Japan for four years and stationed onboard the USS Independence(CV-62). Jim's first book was Go The Distance(2011) and his second book was 2000 Miles on Wisdom(2015). Jim climbed Mt. Fuji and has back packed throughout Asia multiple times. Jim has given numerous speeches on the topics of teamwork and customer service. In 2012 Jim rode a bicycle from Carmel, Indiana to Orlando, Florida to raise money for Multiple Myeloma Cancer. Jim has been married for 16 years to his wife Tarla and they have an 11 year old daughter, Maggie. Family resides in Carmel, Indiana.

For more information about Jim or to contact him, please visit jimserger.com

To line up a speaking engagement please email Jim at, jim@jimserger.com

ABOUT RED BIKE PUBLISHING

Our company is registered as a government contractor company with the CCR and VetBiz (DUNS 826859691). Specifically we are a service disabled veteran owned small business. Red Bike Publishing provides high quality books and include the following which can be found at www.redbikepublishing.com and Amazon.com:

PUBLISHING
Get Rich in a Niche-The Insider's Guide to Self-Publishing in a Specialized Industry ISBN: 978-1-936800-04-9

OTHER TOPICS
1. Rainy Street Stories-Reflections on Secret Wars, Espionage and Terrorism ISBN: 978-1-936800-10-0
2. 2000 Miles On Wisdom ISBN: 978-1-936800-20-9

NOVELS
Commitment-A Novel ASIN: B0057U3GLS
Deovoted ASIN: B015HTZW1K

NATIONAL SECURITY TOPICS
1. DoD Security Clearances and Contracts Guidebook ISBN 978-1-936800-80-3 and ISBN 978-1-936800-99-5
2. Insider's Guide to Security Clearances ISBN: 9781936800988
3. ISP Certification-The Industrial Security Professional Exam Manual ISBN: 9780981620602
4. National Industrial Security Program Operating Manual (NISPOM) ISBN: 978098162060857
5. International Traffic in Arms Regulation (ITAR) ISBN: 97809816288

ARMY TOPICS
1. Ranger Handbook SH 21-76 ISBN-13: 978-1936800087
2. US Army Physical Readiness Training TC 3.22-20 ISBN:97809816240

3. US Army Physical Fitness Training FM 21-20 ISBN:97809816240
4. US Army Leadership FM 6-22 ISBN: 978-0981620671
5. US Army Drill and Ceremonies FM 3-21.5 ISBN: 978-1936800025

www.ingramcontent.com/pod-product-compliance
Lightning Source LLC
Chambersburg PA
CBHW020453100426
42813CB00031B/3352/J